Charles Henry Bell

Phillips Exeter Academy in New Hampshire

A historical sketch

Charles Henry Bell

Phillips Exeter Academy in New Hampshire
A historical sketch

ISBN/EAN: 9783337385842

Printed in Europe, USA, Canada, Australia, Japan

Cover: Foto ©ninafisch / pixelio.de

More available books at **www.hansebooks.com**

PHILLIPS EXETER ACADEMY

IN NEW HAMPSHIRE

A HISTORICAL SKETCH

By CHARLES H. BELL

EXETER, N. H.
WILLIAM B. MORRILL, Printer
News-Letter Press
1883

This sketch has been prepared by the desire of the Trustees of the Academy, in anticipation of the hundredth anniversary of its foundation, and to preserve in the security of print facts liable to perish. It is based in great part on records and other authentic writings ; and though absolute freedom from error is not to be expected, and matters of interest may have been omitted, yet no pains have been spared to avoid mistakes.

The writer acknowledges his obligations to several persons' for information and materials ; and especially to the Rev. Dr. Phillips Brooks, for the loan of correspondence between Dr. John Phillips and his brothers and nephew.

For the opinions expressed in these pages the writer alone is responsible.

PHILLIPS EXETER ACADEMY.

I.

THE FOUNDER.

A hundred years ago, there stood on the Northern side of Water street, nearly opposite the site of the present town hall in Exeter, a somewhat stately dwelling-house, of the architectural style of the olden time, and surmounted with a hipped roof. From time to time afterward it underwent various transformations, none of them for the better, and finally disappeared, within the memory of the present generation, to make way for modern business structures.

This was the Phillips mansion, and its early occupant was the Founder of the Academy, in Exeter, which bears his name.

John Phillips was the second of three sons of the Rev. Samuel Phillips of Andover, Massachusetts, where he was born, December 27, (o. s.) 1719. His great-great-grandfather was the Rev. George Phillips, a native of England and a clergyman, educated at the University of Cambridge, who emigrated to this country in the year 1630, in company with Gov. Winthrop and others. He brought with him his son Samuel, who in due time graduated at Harvard College, and was settled in the ministry at Rowley, Massachusetts, in 1651, and died there after a pastorate of forty-five years, at the age of seventy-one. *His* son Samuel was a goldsmith, and passed his life in Salem, Massachusetts; and left a son Samuel, born there in 1690, a graduate of Harvard College in 1708, the minister of Andover from 1710 to his death in 1771, who was the father of the Exeter Founder.

John Phillips was a promising boy, precocious and fond of learning. Under his father's tuition he was enabled, before he was twelve years of age, to enter Harvard College, and he received his bachelor's degree in 1735, some months before he was sixteen. For a time after his graduation he was employed in teaching a school in his native place, and pursued also the study of medicine and of theology. While yet a young man he was admitted to the ministerial office, and is said to have been esteemed "a devout, zealous, animated and pathetic preacher." Some of the sermons which he prepared were long preserved, and perhaps are still in existence; and there is no doubt that he might have been settled over a parish at an early age, had he not felt a reluctance to it. A delicacy of the lungs is believed to have been a cause of this; and later, after he had listened to the eloquent Whitefield, he felt a distrust of his capacity to realize his ideal of a Christian minister.

He probably first appeared in Exeter, between May and August, 1741, and opened a "private classical school," which he continued for a year or two, and then took charge of the town school for an equal period. He came to be regarded as a permanent inhabitant of the province of New Hampshire in 1743, when his name first appeared upon the list of rate payers. He was then assessed the modest sum of four shillings and two pence; he lived to become the wealthiest citizen of the town.

The same year he took a step which operated to fix his residence permanently in Exeter. He married, on the fourth of August, Mrs. Sarah, "relict" as the phrase was, of Nathaniel Gilman, Esq. She was a daughter of the Rev. Samuel Emery, of Wells, Maine, and was a lady of many virtues, as will appear by a letter of Mr. Phillips to her granddaughter, to be given hereafter.* Mr. Gilman, her first

_____
*Appendix A.

husband, was a person of education, and is credited by tradition with having borne the sobriquet of "Gentleman Nat." He left this widow and three children to inherit a fortune, large for those times, of seventy-five thousand pounds, old tenor. Mr. Phillips at first aspired to marry the eldest daughter, but she preferred another; and thereupon he proposed to the mother, who accepted him. Though there was something of a disparity in their ages, she being forty-one, while he was only twenty-four, yet the marriage was doubtless a very happy one to both parties.

Mr. Phillips soon afterwards entered into mercantile business, in which his industry, economy, methodical habits and sagacity enabled him to gain great success.

Shortly after he made Exeter his home, a new religious society was formed there, of which he became a member. On the twenty-fifth of May, 1747, this society, by a committee of seven prominent members, gave him a pressing invitation to become their pastor, having been, as their letter assured him, "heretofore satisfied of your gracious qualifications, and more lately with your ministerial gifts." This language would indicate that he had already performed some clerical duty for the society; but he was unwilling, for the reasons already mentioned, to assume the responsibilities of a settlement, and declined the invitation. But he long held the office of ruling elder, and as such in 1755 gave his assent, in behalf of the "new gathered church," to the award of a mutual council convened to compose the differences between that and the older religious organization of the town.

Mr. Phillips, as might be supposed from his character and habits, grew ere long to be a man of substance and weight in the community. As he advanced in life there arose premonitory symptoms of serious troubles between the British government and the American colonies. The nullification of the Stamp Act awakened apprehensions, in some minds, of a general prevalence of lawlessness and anarchy; and Mr. Phillips, with others of the principal citizens of Exeter, on the fifteenth of November, 1765, subscribed and published an agreement, to this effect :

"Whereas many evil minded Persons have, on account of the Stamp Act, concluded that all the Laws of this Province and the Execution of the same are at an End,-&c. Therefore we the Subscribers do hereby Combine, Promise and Engage to assemble ourselves together, when and where Need requires, in aid of the Peace Officers, and to Stand by and Defend them in the Execution of their respective Offices, and each other in our respective Properties and Persons, against all Disturbers of the Public Peace and Invaders of Private Property."

Apparently there was in the mind of Mr. Phillips, not far from this time, a question whether he should continue his residence in Exeter. His wife had died on the ninth of October, 1765, and the gathering clouds in the political horizon were alarming to a prudent and well-to-do man. But the repeal of the stamp act the next year, and the appointment of John Wentworth as the governor of the province, gave a more hopeful aspect to the future. Moreover Mr. Phillips determined to enter into a second matrimonial connection. The lady of his choice, whom he married on the third of November, 1767, was Mrs. Elizabeth Hale, widow of Dr. Eliphalet Hale of Exeter, and daughter of the Hon. Ephraim Dennett who had been a prominent citizen of Portsmouth and a mandamus Councillor. This lady is represented as possessing most estimable qualities ; she was a prudent, helpful and devoted wife to Mr. Phillips, whom she survived but two or three years.*

He now began to be invested with offices and trusts which in those days conferred no small distinction. Gov. Wentworth caused his name to be inserted in the Commission of the Peace as early as 1768, and continued it there as long as the royal government endured in the province. In 1771, 1772 and 1773 he was elected a Representative from Exeter

*Mrs. Phillips died in September, 1797.

in the provincial assembly. From 1772 to 1775 he sat as a Judge of the Inferior Court of Common Pleas ; and toward the close of Gov. Wentworth's administration he is understood to have received the appointment of mandamus Councillor, but it does not appear that he ever acted in that capacity.

Gov. Wentworth, who was of a conciliatory disposition, and fond of military parade, proposed to Mr. Phillips in 1770 the formation of a *corps d'elite*, to embrace many of the principal citizens of Exeter, and to act as a body guard of the chief magistrate. The plan was carried into effect, and Mr. Phillips received the appointment of commander, with the rank of Colonel. Nothing was spared to give distinction to the corps. It was called by the name of the Exeter Cadets : the uniform of scarlet and buff was rich and handsome, the cocked hats, and ruffles at the bosom and wrists gave an air of superiority, at that time when dress meant so much. The officers appeared in all the bravery of gorget and sash, with sword and spontoon ; and a handsome stand of colors rendered the equipment of the company complete.

In September, 1770, his excellency the Governor, his lady and suite were present at the publishing of the commissions of the officers, and dined at the house of Col. Phillips. Again in 1772 the Governor attended a parade of "his Cadets," as he called them, and declared himself much gratified therewith. Col. Phillips performed his military duties with strict fidelity, and his command was often called together for exercise, and was in an admirable state of discipline. But it contained a considerable proportion of those who, when the impending revolution summoned men to take sides, became "high sons of liberty," and on the morning after the memorable day of Concord and Lexington, a goodly number of the Cadets marched off for Cambridge, without orders from their commander, carrying on their shoulders the bright muskets which the royal governor had provided. to swell the

ranks of the army of colonists who initiated the siege of
Boston.

Although Col. Phillips was chosen by his townsmen in
1774 a member of the Committee of Correspondence, yet it
is certain that he took no active part in the American Revolution. Nor was this strange. Men situated as he was are
not the stuff of which revolutions are made. He had been
educated in a reverence for authority, and had felt no hard-
ship from the rule of the mother country such as to justify
resistance to it. He was in mature life, with an easy fortune and an assured position. He had nothing to gain, but
everything to lose, by a change of government.

It is time that the indiscriminate prejudice which has so
long prevailed against the loyalists of the Revolution, should
give place to more just and rational views. The men who
adhered to the crown from selfish or interested motives, and
contrary to their own sense of right, may indeed be justly
despised ; but those whose motives were honorable and
whose attachment to the mother country was genuine, con-
stituting a large proportion of the loyalists of the North at
least, deserve no stigma for acting with the courage of their
convictions. Col. Phillips however, could not be justly ac-
counted as a "tory." "From principle he disapproved of
the Revolution, but made no active opposition to it. He was
solicitous to preserve a state of neutrality in the contest,
and studiously avoided conversation on the subject, and, as
far as he was able, everything relating to it."*

About the time of the breaking out of the Revolution, Col.
Phillips ceased trading, and employed that part of his property which was not vested in land, in making loans on interest. By this time he had gathered much wealth, and as he had
neither children nor needy relatives, it became a serious problem with him what ultimate disposition he should make of
it. It was not a new question. Descended from a line of
clergymen, educated in all religious observances, and a pro-

*MS. of Gov. Plumer.

fessor of christianity from the age of fifteen, he had been always accustomed to regard his property as accompanied with a sacred trust. As early as when he was a teacher of youth, he had recorded in his private memoranda this resolution: "Being sensible that a part of my income is required of me to be spent in the more immediate service of God, I therefore devote a tenth of my salary for keeping school, to pious and charitable purposes."* And among the fragments of his correspondence which have come down to our time, are two letters, one to each of his brothers, Samuel at Andover, and William at Boston, both of whom were in prosperous circumstances, which indicate how steadily the idea of dedicating a portion of his possessions to benevolent and charitable uses dwelt in his mind.†

The first considerable gifts which were made by Col. Phillips in pursuance of this design, of which we have any definite information, were to the infant Dartmouth College. The Rev. Dr. Eleazer Wheelock, who had been at the head of the Indian Charity School in Connecticut, was about removing it into New Hampshire, there to be erected by royal charter into a college. Col. Phillips in 1770 subscribed a considerable tract of land,—seven rights in the new township of Sandwich,—to the funds of the institution, upon the condition that it should be established at Hanover; which was done. Two years afterwards he gave to the college the sum of £175, lawful money, for the purchase of a philosophical apparatus, and the next year the further sum of £125, to aid in "furthering the great purpose of the institution," which was, primarily though by no means exclusively, the education and christianization of the American Indians. In the year 1781 he conveyed to the Trustees upwards of 4000 acres of land, situated in several townships in Northern New Hampshire and in Vermont, to be held for the use of the College, with-

*MS. of Gov. Plumer.
†Appendix B.

out restrictions; and finally, in 1789 he added the sum of
£37 10s. upon condition that the College should contribute lands to an equal amount, to be consolidated with
his former donation of lands, for the foundation of a professorship of Divinity. The endowment thus constituted is
still known by his name, and yields an annual income of
about $400.

Col. Phillips was chosen a trustee of Dartmouth College
in 1773, and performed the duties of the position with much
interest and punctuality until his resignation, by reason of
years and bodily infirmity, in 1793. In 1777, the College conferred upon him the honorary degree of Doctor of Laws.
This was the second instance in which the institution had
granted that mark of distinction, the other being in the case
of Gov. John Wentworth, "the father of the College," who
received it in 1773.

The next educational enterprise,* which engaged the attention, and received the benefactions of Dr. Phillips, was the
planting of the Academy in his native town. In the year
1777 the Hon. Samuel Phillips, Jr., of Andover, his nephew,
being familiar, no doubt, with the long cherished intentions
of his uncle and father, to make some special charitable use
of a portion of the fortunes which they had acquired, project-
ed the school which was afterwards incorporated as the
Phillips Andover Academy. The brothers John and Samuel
Phillips jointly endowed it, in 1778, with the means to begin
its work, and Dr. Phillips afterwards, by gift and by bequest, increased his gratuities to the institution to the amount
of about $31,000, thereby becoming its chief benefactor. He
served as one of the Trustees of that Academy during his life,
and after the death of his eldest brother, as President, and
displayed an interest in its affairs and management only
less lively and active than that which he felt in the latest and

---

*He is said also to have made donations to Princeton and to
Harvard College, and to have given money to aid the cause of education, to towns in the vicinity of his home.

most important work of benevolence, which crowned his useful career.

This was Phillips Exeter Academy, which was exclusively Dr. Phillips' own project. To the foundation and upbuilding of this institution he consecrated the greater part of his fortune, besides giving to it his personal supervision as President of the board of Trustees during the last twelve years of his life. His rare judgment of men and his cultivated business capacity well supplemented the far reaching wisdom of his plans, and the Academy prospered in its resources and in its work. The Founder lived to see it established on a firm basis, and giving assurance of that extended measure of usefulness which later generations have witnessed.

This great mission accomplished, he felt that his life work was finished. He had considerably passed the ordinary period of man's earthly existence, and was ready to be called hence. His closing hours were thus described by one who knew him well.*

"His last illness was very short. He was seized with a kind of fainting fit on Monday morning, from which he in part recovered, so as to walk about the house, and was perfectly sensible and apprised of his approaching dissolution, and spake of it to his friends with calmness and serenity, and with apparent pleasure. And, according to information, expressed himself in words to this effect : ' My work is done, I have settled all my affairs, and have now nothing to do but to die ; it is no matter how soon.' And retaining his reason to the last, the next morning he died, April the 21st, 1795, in the seventy-sixth year of his age."

All suitable honors were paid to his memory. The Trustees of Phillips Exeter Academy chose one of their number, the Rev. Benjamin Thurston, to pronounce a eulogy upon the Founder, at the next annual meeting of the board ; a duty which he duly performed to their approval. They also

*The Rev. Jonathan French, in a sermon preached on the occasion of the death of Dr. Phillips, at Andover, Massachusetts.

voted that a copy of Dr. Phillips' portrait "elegantly decorat-
ed" should be taken and placed in the Library of the Academy.

The body of Dr. Phillips rests in the cemetery of the town
in which the most important share of his life was passed, and
upon the marble monument which his associates in the trust
caused to be erected over it, is inscribed an appropriate epitaph, composed by the accomplished Nathaniel A. Haven, Jr.*

A biography which records only the public acts and exter-
nal life of its subject, is necessarily bare and unsatisfactory.
No one feels that he knows another, thoroughly, until he is
acquainted with his inner qualities, his private, domestic relations, his personal peculiarities. An anecdote often throws
more light on character than an essay.

It is to be regretted that so few memorials of Dr. Phillips'
private life have descended to our time. There are sufficient
data perhaps to give us an idea of the Founder; but of John
Phillips the man, we unfortunately have few authentic materials from which to fashion any adequate portraiture.

It is certain that he was not a popular favorite. The
children disliked to meet him because he so rigorously ex-
acted from them the outward marks of respect to which he
thought his years and position entitled him;† for he was
bred in a school in which reverence for superiors was insisted on as the imperative duty of the young. His neighbors,
although they entertained for him a distant respect, evidently did not love him. By nature and by habit he was reserved
and formal, and he had neither the ready adaptability that
interests its possessor in the concerns of others, nor those
companionable qualities which are so much valued by one's

*Appendix C. A terse, and strikingly just epitaph proposed
for him was,—"Without natural issue he made posterity his heir."
†A venerable lady of Exeter states that it was Dr. Phillips' habit in his later years, to pace up and down the platform before his
house, and to insist that every boy who passed, should doff the
hat, and every girl make a courtesy, to him.
Professor Hoyt relates that "he would not give a boy a cherry
from his trees, unless the favor were asked with a low bow, and
in the most reverent tone."

associates. And, worst of all. he was wealthy,—a money lender,—frugal and saving to the very verge of parsimony. Little wonder that traditions of niggardliness and of hard treatment of the poor, should have sprung up about such a man.*

But beneath that cold exterior there beat a warm and benevolent heart. The fragments of his correspondence that remain, show the cordiality of his affection for those connected with him by the ties of consanguinity, and his thorough appreciation of the womanly charms and virtues that rendered his home happy. His secret sympathies, too, went out in an ever widening circle, to every creature in poverty and ignorance, struggling for the light. He did not amass riches for his own enjoyment or aggrandizement; still less for the avaricious pleasure of possession; else he could never have brought himself to part with the control of them during his life, and especially after the age of acquisition was passed. He had a high and noble motive for his accumulations. He saved on principle, that he might give the more wisely and effectively. His generosity sprang from no shallow momentary impulse, nor were his thousands lavished for the sake of popularity or notoriety. The charity that enshrines his name was self-denying, systematic, catholic and of highest purpose.

The painted portrait of Dr. Phillips in the possessio of the Academy, attributed to the characterizing brush of Stuart. bears an expression of kindness and benevolence, blended with shrewdness and sagacity. Apparently it represents faithfully his leading characteristics. The Hon. Josiah Quincy, his connection by marriage, who in his youth knew Dr. Phillips well, asserts that "he should never forget the patriarchial sweetness of his countenance." And it is the testimony of the Rev. Dr. Abiel Abbot, the historian of Andover, also a personal acquaintance. that Dr. Phillips was "a saga-

*Mr. Wendell Phillips is authority for the statement that an old woman who had lived in the family of Dr. Phillips, said—"he was a good man,—and he always soaked his back-logs in water over night!"

cious observer of human nature, shrewd in his remarks ; seldom erred in judgment, and had much practical wisdom."

He has sometimes been represented as belonging to the sourest sect of puritans ; and it is true that he clung tenaciously to the narrow and rigid religious tenets in which he had been educated ; but it was with the intellect far more than with the heart. In his practice he was in advance of his time, in respect to religious tolerance. It was well said of him that "his austere faith was softened by natural temperament and by inherent kindliness of spirit." He certainly was ready to appreciate goodness wherever he found it,, and even if interwoven with religious dogmas which he could not accept. The major part of his associates on the board of trust, and the first Principal of the Academy, all not only approved but nominated by himself, held theological views to a greater or less extent at variance with his own.

On the whole it may be said of Dr. Phillips that his foibles were few and venial, while his virtues were numerous and shining. He is entitled, not to the questionable commendation of having "builded better than he knew," but to rank with those benefactors of mankind, whose building, because it was perfected at the cost of much study and sacrifice. filled out the exact measure of their wishes.

II.

The Academy; 1781 to 1838.

Phillips Exeter Academy was incorporated by the Legislature of New Hampshire, by an Act which received the approval of the President of the State, the third of April, 1781. It was a wise step on the part of Dr. Phillips to begin this educational experiment in his lifetime, and while he was yet of an age to take an active part in its direction. There was little experience in the management of similar institutions for him to profit by ; he was entering upon a field that was almost untrodden. The only precedents for his guidance were to be drawn from the Phillips Andover Academy, which had been chartered but a year before, and from the Dummer Academy at Byfield, Massachusetts, which, though it had been in operation eighteen years, was yet unincorporated. Accordingly the responsibility of shaping the project in its inception, and of giving it the direction which was to conduct it to ultimate success, fell chiefly upon the Founder, who fortunately possessed the knowledge and experience and foresight which admirably qualified him for the task.

The Act of Incorporation provided "that there be, and hereby is, established in the Town of Exeter and County of Rockingham, an Academy for the purpose of promoting Piety and Virtue, and for the education of youth in the English, Latin and Greek Languages, in Writing, Arithmetic, Music and the Art of Speaking, Practical Geometry, Logic and Geography, and such other of the Liberal Arts and Sciences or Languages, as opportunity may hereafter permit, and as the

Trustees hereinafter provided, shall direct." The control and government of the Academy were by the Act vested in a board of Trustees, not more than seven nor less than four in number, of whom one should be the principal instructor, a majority should be laymen, and a majority not inhabitants of Exeter. The Trustees were empowered to fill all vacancies that should occur in their own board; and by a vote of two thirds of their whole number, to remove the Academy from Exeter, if for causes thereafter arising that course should, upon mature consideration, be found needful, and establish it in some other place in the State which they should "judge best calculated for carrying into effectual execution the intention of the Founder." And, finally, the Act of Incorporation stipulated "that all the lands, tenements and personal estate, that shall be given to the Trustees for the use of said Academy, shall be, and hereby are, forever exempted from all taxes whatsoever."*

The first board of Trustees was composed of the following gentlemen : Dr. John Phillips, the Hon. Samuel Phillips, Jr., of Andover, Massachusetts, Thomas Odiorne, Esq., of Exeter, the Hon. John Pickering, LL. D., of Portsmouth, the Rev. David McClure, of North Hampton, and Major Daniel Tilton, and the Rev. Benjamin Thurston, both of Exeter. The last named gentleman was expected to be the principal teacher of the school, and in point of fact, if tradition is to be relied upon, did give instruction in it for a time, before the formal opening of the Academy.

On the ninth day of January, 1782, Dr. Phillips completed a conveyance to the Trustees for the use of the Academy, of his interest in a large number of tracts of land, sit-

---

*Some alarmist, having with perverse ingenuity insisted that by virtue of this provision all property which had once been held by the Academy would be forever after freed from taxation to subsequent owners, the Trustees, by petition to the Legislature, procured the passage of an Act declaring that the exemption from taxation was to continue only so long as the property should belong to the Academy.

uated in various towns in New Hampshire, some of which he
owned in fee, and others were under mortgage to him to secure the payment of moneys due. Although we have not
the means to compute the value of this gift, yet it undoubtedly was sufficient to meet all the probable requirements of
the Academy, for making a successful beginning, at least.

In his deed of conveyance Dr. Phillips embodied a series
of standing regulations, which he termed the "Constitution"
of the Academy, and which he directed should be read at
each annual meeting of the Trustees. It contained somewhat minute definitions of the duties of the several officers,
which were less familiar then than now, as well as many
practical suggestions of lasting value. The rule was there
inculcated, which has always since been adhered to with sig-
nal advantage, that no pupil should board in any family not
licensed by the authorities of the Academy. The only restrictions of a religious character in the instrument were that
the Trustees and teachers must be Protestants ; and that the
principal instructor should be a member of the Church of
Christ, in complete standing, and professing sentiments similar to those of the Founder in the Constitution expressed.
The Founder also reserved to himself the power to appoint
his successor in the board of trust, who, as well as his suc-
cessors after him, should enjoy the same right forever. This
Constitution has of course been the constant guide of the
Trustees from that time to the present, in the execution of
their functions.

Dr. Phillips added to the resources of the Academy by
repeated acts of generosity, afterwards. On the twenty-ninth
of March, 1787, he made an assignment to the Trustees, of
promissory notes against various parties, to the amount of
£4,161 or thereabout ; and on the twenty-fifth day of November, 1789, another assignment of property of a similar nature, the value of which is not stated, for the special purpose
of affording aid to charity scholars "such as may be of ex-
celling genius and of good moral character." And by his

last will, executed in 1789 and proved in 1795, he devised two thirds of the residue of his estate, after small bequests to his relatives, and a rather slender provision for his widow,* to Phillips Exeter Academy; the other third being given to the Academy at Andover.

The various benefactions of Dr. Phillips to the Exeter Academy are estimated to amount in the aggregate to about $60,-000. In the present era of vast acquiring and magnificent giving, there is danger of undervaluing the bounty expressed by these comparatively modest figures. We need to bear in mind that the worth of money, one hundred years ago, was four fold greater than it is to-day; that the Founder devoted to this object the major part of the accumulations of a laborious and extraordinarily successful life; and that no endowment of a similar enterprise in the country up to that time, approached this in magnitude. And, finally, in order to estimate the value of the foundation aright, it is necessary to consider what has since been accomplished by it; to look down the long line of alumni who have been enabled, through the facilities which it has afforded, to attain distinguished places in every important walk of life; and to weigh the impetus which it has thus given to the scholarship, the literature, and the professional and business progress of the country and of the age.

The charter for the Academy obtained, and the necessary funds provided, the next step was to determine the location of the Academy building. And here arose a difference of opinion, as has so often been the case in the settlement of like questions. Dr. Phillips, though apparently holding a pretty decided opinion on the point, had the wisdom not to take sides, and it was decided to place the school house on a spot somewhat westerly of the present site of the Acade-

---

*The provision for Mrs. Phillips was increased, from the estate, to her entire satisfaction, by the joint action of the Exeter and Andover Academies, in the proportion to their several interests in the residuum.

my, and on the opposite side of what is now called Academy street, but is better known to the older Alumni by the less elegant name of "Tan lane." A modest edifice was accordingly erected there, and was probably made ready for occupation, in part at least, early in the year 1783.

As Mr. Thurston's health was found to be insufficient to admit of his assuming the office of preceptor, it next became necessary to choose a person for that position. After due inquiry, William Woodbridge, A. B., of Glastonbury, Connecticut, a graduate of Yale College in 1780, was selected.

It was thought fitting that the inauguration of this new seminary of learning, founded on a scale of unprecedented liberality, should be accompanied by public observances ; accordingly the Trustees appointed the Rev. David McClure, one of their own number, to deliver a discourse on the opening of the Academy, and the Rev. Benjamin Thurston to make an address to the new preceptor, on his induction into office.

The first of May, 1783, was designated for the ceremonies, "and on that day," says a contemporary record, "the Hon. Founder and Trustees, with many other gentlemen and a respectable auditory, attended in one of the meeting-houses in this town. The exercises began with singing, a prayer succeeded by the Rev. Mr. Rogers, and an Oration on the advantages of Learning and its happy Tendency to promote Virtue and Piety, was delivered by Rev. David McClure, A. M., with an Address to the Founder, Trustees and Preceptor. The inaugurating ceremonies were performed by Mr. Thurston, a gentleman of the trust, with a particular address and charge to the Preceptor. Mr. Woodbridge, the Preceptor, then publicly manifested his acceptance of the important charge, and pronounced an affectionate address to the Trustees and auditory. A prayer was made by the Rev. Mr. Mansfield, and the whole was concluded by singing. Each part was performed with propriety and the solemnity suitable to the occasion; the whole to universal acceptance."*

In view of what the school has since grown to be, it is rather a striking contrast to look back to the humble pretensions of its infancy.

An unobtrusive school-house of two stories, of the dimensions of a small dwelling, and divided into four rooms, not all of which were finished, supplied limited accommodation for forty students—sometimes a much smaller number, and this though the tuition was gratuitous,—of whom two-thirds, at least, belonged in Exeter, and scarcely any out of its immediate vicinity. The preceptor's salary was £100 per annum, and the compensation of his single assistant was proportionally less. There was no regular course of study, but the pupils pursued such branches and formed such classes, as were found most convenient. It was thought worthy of mention in the records, that a bell "to summon the students to their exercises" was presented in 1784 by Gen. Henry Dearborn of revolutionary fame, and other gentlemen of Exeter; and that an electrical machine was given by the Hon. Phillips White, of South Hampton. Such petty charges as the cost of wood and candles were apportioned by a tax among the students, and he who did not pay his share, forfeited the privileges of the Academy until his deficiency was made good. And as late as in 1788 we learn that there were but two pupils in the school who had "looked beyond common reading and spelling, into the mysteries of Latin." Truly this was the day of small things.†

Mr. Woodbridge continued to act as Preceptor of the Academy something over five years. In June, 1788, he announc-

---

*Mr. McClure's oration was published at the time, together with the charter of the Academy, in a 4to. pamphlet. It was an excellent production, though not exactly brilliant. No better illustration could be given of the change which a century has wrought in men's ideas of the requirements of such an occasion, than the comment of an eloquent divine of our day, after reading the oration:—"I rejoice to know that there was a time when men dared to be dull."

†Appendix D.

ed to the Trustees his intention of resigning his position in the ensuing October, because of his "low state of health." There is reason also to think that the dwindling of the number of new pupils during the later years of his stay, somewhat discouraged Mr. Woodbridge in his hopes of building up a great school.

Inquiry was therefore set on foot for some one with the needful qualifications to supply the place of Mr. Woodbridge. Fortunately the Trustees succeeded, with little delay, in finding a young man whose subsequent career showed him to have a wonderful adaptation for the duties required of him. Sometime in August, 1788, Benjamin Abbot, a native of Andover, Massachusetts, and a graduate of Harvard College of that year, was secured for the preceptorship of the Academy, and on the twenty-second or twenty-third of the same month entered upon the duties of instruction and government of the school ;* Mr. Woodbridge rarely visiting it afwards, although his connection was not formally severed until the fourteenth of October following. Here commenced those relations between Benjamin Abbot and Phillips Exeter Academy which endured for half a century, with the result of elevating the institution to a rank unsurpassed in this country, and of making its master, as an educator and governor of youth, an exemplar even to our own time.

The prospects of the school began at once to brighten. Order and method were introduced. The young preceptor infused his own quiet force into the boys under his charge, and the results were soon manifest in the increase of their numbers. In the first year after Mr. Abbot's arrival as many new pupils were admitted as had been added in the three preceding years. But he was a man of singular prudence, and declined to connect himself permanently with the school until he had proved his value. It was not until October, 1791, that he formally signified his acceptance of the office of Preceptor, and this upon the understanding with the

---

*MS. letter of Charles Folsom.

Trustees that either party should be at liberty to dissolve the connection, upon giving reasonable notice. His salary was raised to the sum of five hundred dollars per annum, and his assistant, John P. Ripley A. B., received two hundred dollars.

In a very few years the situation of the Academy demanded an increase of accommodations for the students. The original building was small and unsuitable, and the need of a larger and more commodious one became pressing, as the school augmented. It was, therefore, determined in 1793 to erect "a new building for the use of the Academy."

The committee for carrying the plan into execution was judiciously constituted of two members of the board of Trustees, the Hon. Samuel Phillips, Jr., and the Preceptor ; the Treasurer, the Hon. John Taylor Gilman ; and two public spirited citizens of the town, the Hon. Oliver Peabody and Col. Nathaniel Gilman. They were empowered to procure a building to be erected, of certain specified dimensions on the ground ; of the height of two stories ; the materials to be brick or wood ; and "with or without a porch and belfry as the committee, after advising with the Trustees present, should judge best." The location of the building was wisely left to the determination of the committee, with the concurrence of the resident Trustees.

The new edifice was completed in the year 1794. It was constructed of wood, with a belfry and without a portico, and at a cost of between seven and ten thousand dollars. With some additions at a later period, it fulfilled its purpose well until the generation which witnessed its building had, with scarce an exception, passed off the stage.

Dr. Phillips, who survived to see the institution he had planted, flourishing with a healthful and secure growth, died in 1795. In the execution of the power he had reserved to himself in the Consitution, to name his successor in the board of trust, he had by a written appointment designated the Hon. John Taylor Gilman for the office, who accepted it, and long and assiduously performed its duties.

In March, 1797, it was voted by the Trustees that any student who had been a member of the Academy for six months and should appear on examination "to have made valuable improvement in the Latin and Greek languages, Arithmetic, practical Geometry, Logic, Geography, Philosophy and Astronomy," or in any two or more of those studies, and had sustained a good moral character, should be entitled to a certificate thereof, signed by the President and Preceptor, with the seal of the Academy affixed thereto.

There is extant, in the youthful handwriting of Lewis Cass,—in after years the distinguished Senator, Foreign Minister and Cabinet Officer,—a copy of the certificate which was granted to him by virtue of the foregoing vote, on his leaving the Academy. It is in these words:

"PHILLIPS EXETER ACADEMY.

"The Trustees of Phillips Exeter Academy, with a view to encourage Industry, Science and Morality, have determined that certificates may be granted to students in certain cases. Be it therefore known that Lewis Cass has been a member of the said Academy seven years, and appears on examination to have acquired the principles of the English, French, Latin and Greek languages, Geography, Arithmetic and practical Geometry; that he has made very valuable progress in the study of Rhetoric, History, Natural and Moral Philosophy, Logic, Astronomy and Natural Law; and that he has sustained a good moral character during said term.

"In testimony whereof we hereunto set our hands, and affix the seal of said Academy, this second day of October, one thousand seven hundred and ninety-nine.

"JOHN T. GILMAN.
"BENJAMIN ABBOT."

This certificate sheds some light upon the fashions of work done in the Academy at that early day. Lewis Cass was born in 1782; he therefore became a pupil when he was ten, and quitted the school when he was seventeen years of age.

That there could have been any curriculum embracing a seven years' course of study is out of the question; he must therefore have pursued his way alone, or in such company as chance from time to time brought him. The range of subjects, too, was certainly for the time, very remarkable; a fortunate circumstance for Cass, who had little opportunity afterwards to add to his academic training.

In the year 1808 a very decided forward step was taken in the organization of the Academy. The qualifications for admission with a view to an English education were defined, and apparently considerably raised; the head master was vested with the title of Principal; a professorship of Mathematics and Natural Philosophy was established, with a competent salary; it was voted expedient to reduce the number of classes and to establish a uniform system of classification, to be effected by the Principal and Professor; and an appropriation of fifty dollars annually was made, to be distributed in the shape of rewards or prizes to those students who should excel in Mathematics, Writing, English composition, and in knowledge of Latin.*   Ebenezer Adams, A. M. was chosen as the first Professor.

Up to this time all the instruction in the Academy had been furnished to the pupils gratuitously, the only charges upon them being some trifling contributions for special purposes. But in the year 1809, the Trustees, in view of the increasing expenses of the institution, in accordance with the known expectations of the Founder, and in order that they might be enabled to extend aid to the usual number of students on the foundation, voted that it was necessary to require payment from those of sufficient ability, for their tuition. This change however, it was found expedient to postpone until the first of January, 1812; after which date the sum of twelve dollars per year, or three dollars per term, became payable, for tuition.

The mansion house on Water street, in which Dr. Phillips

_____
*Appendix E.

had resided, came into the possession of the Academy upon the death of his widow, and was occupied by the Principal until about 1811. A year or two previously the Trustees had caused a dwelling house to be built for the use of Professor Adams, nearly opposite the Academy grounds ; but as he soon afterwards left the town, Dr. Abbot became its first occupant, while the Rev. Hosea Hildreth, who in 1811 succeeded Professor Adams in the Mathematical chair, took possession of the Phillips house.*

In 1817 the Rev. Isaac Hurd, then about to be settled over the second parish in Exeter, received the appointment of Instructor in Theology. It had been unquestionably the original expectation of the Founder to make theological instruction a part of the regular course in the Academy ; with the idea, possibly, that a seminary for the education of students for the religious ministry would eventually grow out of it, as has been the case in the sister institution at Andover. Accordingly, in 1790, during Dr. Phillips' lifetime, the Rev. Joseph Buckminster was elected, by the Trustees, Professor of Divinity in the Academy, with a salary equal to that of the Preceptor. But he declined the office.

No other person was chosen in his stead ; but for many years afterwards appropriations were made by the Trustees from time to time, of moneys to defray the expenses of students in divinity, who pursued their studies under the direction of neighboring clergymen, such as the Rev. Jesse Appleton, of Hampton, the Rev. Joseph Buckminster, of Portsmouth, and the Rev. Daniel Dana, of Newburyport,

---

*It is related, as an indication of the change which time produces even in small places, that Dr. Abbot and his family removed to their new abode with reluctance, because, besides being in the midst of the sands, it was out of the way of all their friends and neighbors. Exeter has since yielded to the law that "all towns grow to the westward," and the house is now nearly in the centre of her inhabitants. In the more than seventy years of its existence, it has sheltered but two families,—those of the first two Principals. The venerable widow of Dr. Soule occupied it up to the time of her decease, the ninth day of May, 1883.

who were named by the Trustees as committees for the purpose.

It may be added here that no further attempt was made during the life of the Founder, or afterwards, to establish a professorship of Divinity, and that Mr. Hurd ceased to hold the post of Theological Instructor in the year 1839. Since that time there has been no special teacher of religious science in the Academy, but it has been treated as the duty of the regular instructors to "form the Morals,"—to use the language of the "Constitution,"—as well as to "enlarge the Minds of the youth committed to their care."

The standing and popular estimate of the Academy had, in the year 1818, risen so high that it became necessary to define anew the course of study, to draw a strict line of distinction between the English and classical departments, and to adopt more stringent regulations in respect to the reception of pupils.

Candidates for admission were required thenceforth to furnish evidence of their good moral character, and to give assurance of their intention to remain at the Academy until they should complete the usual routine of preparation for college, or the established course of English study. The time fixed for their admission was at the beginning of the term next succeeding the annual meeting of the Trustees in August; provided, however, that any one found duly qualified, might be received at advanced standing, at the discretion of the instructors. The department of languages was to comprise three classes, or years, for preparation to enter college, and an advanced class to prosecute the studies of the first collegiate year. The course of English study was also to occupy three years. Theological instruction was to be given by the Rev. Mr. Hurd, and sacred music was to be taught, a fund of $1000 having been bequeathed by the Hon. Nicholas Gilman in 1814, the income of which was to be applied to that object. A permanent assistant teacher was also engaged, at an annual salary of six hundred dollars.

The particular studies and text books for each year. both in the classical and the English course. were at this time specifically designated, and will be given in the Appendix. for the purpose of comparison with the work required at the present day.*

In 1821, the convenient accommodation of the students requiring additional space in the school building, wings of a single story were affixed to the eastern and western ends thereof, each containing a school room of ample size. They added much to the symmetry of the structure. as well as to its convenience ; and the appearance of the building as thus extended, is well remembered by most of the older Alumni.

Thus improved in organization and in accommodations, the Academy for years kept on the even tenor of its way. ever changing. yet the same. The number of students was usually fixed at seventy, and varied little from it. At length Dr. Abbot.—he had received the degree of Doctor of Laws, *honoris causa*, from Dartmouth College in 1811,—who was blessed with a vigorous constitution and up to this time had enjoyed almost uninterrupted health, began to feel the effects of his long continued labors and responsibilities : and in the year 1832 made application to the board of Trustees for some respite or relief, submitting to them the question whether his resignation would be acceptable. They were unwilling that he should sunder his connection with the Academy, and made an arrangement with him, whereby by lessening the number of students, and confining them rigidly to the fixed classes, the Principal was relieved of a portion of his labor. This arrangement continued until 1836, when at the request of Dr. Abbot an additional instructor was appointed, for the purpose of exempting him from the larger portion of his active duties. For the last year or two of his service as Principal his attendance at recitations was limited to two quarters of days in each week.

The close of the half century of Dr. Abbot's charge of the

*Appendix F.

school now drew near, and by the desire of many of his old
pupils he postponed his retirement until that period should
be completed. All united in the opinion that the termination of a career so long and so signally honorable and useful
should be marked by public manifestations worthy of the occasion. A Committee of Arrangements, consisting of a number of gentlemen of note, Alumni of the Academy, made all
the needful preparations for holding what was appropriately
termed the "Abbot Festival," and appointed the twenty-third
of August, 1838, as the day of its occurrence.

It was an event to be remembered by every one who witnessed it. A beautiful summer day enabled all to enjoy the
exercises without discomfort, and the number of persons assembled, considering the limited means of transportation at
that date, was surprising. It was estimated that nearly four
hundred of the Alumni were present, besides a scarcely less
number of strangers who had not enjoyed the privileges of
the institution.

At eleven o'clock in the forenoon, in accordance with the
programme, a meeting of the Alumni was held, in the Academy yard, about the eastern wing of the building. Daniel
Webster was appointed chairman, and Charles Folsom and
Oliver W. B. Peabody, Secretaries. The exercises were
opened with a prayer by the Rev. Dr. John G. Palfrey. Mr.
Webster then explained in a brief and impressive address
the object of the meeting, and read the communication of
Dr. Abbot to the Trustees, in which he apprised them of his
intention to retire from the office of Principal, and their response thereto.* He also read an interesting letter from the
Rev. Dr. Daniel Dana, of Newburyport, long a member of the
board of Trustees, who was unable to be present on the occasion.

The Hon. Leverett Saltonstall, chairman of the Committee
of Arrangements, then submitted a report in their behalf.
He said their efforts had been directed to four several ends,

*Appendix G.

all designed to do honor to the venerated Principal on his surrender of the duties which he had discharged so long and so ably ;—first, to secure a gathering of the Alumni, at the Abbot Festival ; second, to obtain a painted portrait of Dr. Abbot, to be placed in the Academy ; third, to procure a handsome piece of plate to be presented to him as a token of respect from his old pupils ; and fourth, to found and endow a permanent scholarship in Harvard College, as a memorial of Dr. Abbot, and to bear his name. All these purposes the Committee had succeeded in accomplishing, except the last. and they had the assurance that in due time that also would be effected.

The Report concluded with a Resolution expressing in terms of gratitude and affectionate regard the sense entertained by the meeting of the inestimable value of the faithful and long continued services of Dr. Abbot. The Resolution was advocated with feeling and eloquence by the Rev. Henry Ware, Jr., Gov. Edward Everett,* the Rev. Dr. Palfrey, Judge Peter O. Thacher, and the Hon. Jonathan Chapman, and was unanimously adopted.

At the close of these preliminary exercises the Alumni repaired to the hall of the Academy, and there paid their res· pects to the venerable recipient of the honors of the day.

At the hour of half-past one in the afternoon a procession was formed and marshalled to the dinner table. A blessing was asked by the Rev. Dr. John H. Morison. After the meat, Mr. Webster, who presided, addressed the company in an appropriate, eloquent and touching manner. It is much to be regretted that his remarks, which occupied an hour in the delivery, were not reported with sufficient fulness to give us any adequate idea of their scope or merit. From the journals of the day this imperfect account is obtained.

"We have often heard Mr. Webster, but never on any

*Gov. Everett's remarks on this occasion are reported in full, in his elegant, expansive style, in one of the volumes of his collected works.

occasion when he appeared to better advantage than on this. He was emphatically eloquent and truly himself. He not only drew tears from the venerable man in whose honor we had assembled, but from very many of the numerous audience."

"He recalled the attention of the assembly to the objects for which they had met. He recurred to the services which had been rendered, during his long term of arduous duty, by their respected friend now retiring from the field of active service ; passed a glowing eulogium upon the character and worth of the accomplished instructors of youth of whom he described their friend as a conspicuous example : and dwelt at considerable length in a series of just remarks and forcible illustrations, upon the importance to the welfare of the community of judicious systems of instruction, and the labors of able and faithful instructors of youth. He concluded by an affectionate address in the name of his fellow students to their Preceptor, and by presenting him a piece of plate (which had in the meantime been placed before him,) as a token of their regard."*

This was an elegant and massive vase of silver, bearing an inscription commemorative of the occasion.

Dr. Abbot rose to reply. Foreseeing that the trying nature of his position would incapacitate him for making an

*In the process of arranging the considerable collection of Mr. Webster's papers, presented after his death by the Hon. Peter Harvey to the New Hampshire Historical Society, a couple of folded sheets were found bearing the indorsement,—"Exeter Academy Celebration." It was a disappointment to find that when opened they contained not even the heads of Mr. Webster's address, but only the two following Latin quotations which he undoubtedly introduced therein, and which were singularly apposite to the occasion.

"Arcebat cum ab illecebris peccantium, præter ipsius bonam integramque naturam, quod statim parvulus sedem ac magistram studiorum Massiliam habuit, locum Græca comitate et provinciali parsimonia mixtum ac bene compositum."

"Mihi ille detur puer quem laus excitet, quem gloria juvet, qui victus fleat. Hic erit alendus ambitu, hunc mordebit objurgatio, hunc honor excitabit, in hoc desidiam nunquam verebor."

extemporaneous response, he had committed what he wished
to say, to writing ; but he found when the critical moment
arrived, that his emotions were too great for utterance. Gov.
Everett with ready sympathy came to his relief. "Breth-
ren," said he, "the voice that has never failed for a day, in
fifty years' teaching, now falters ;" and receiving the manu-
script from his old master's hand, he read its contents, with
characteristic grace and impressiveness, to the assembly. As
might have been expected from their author, Dr. Abbot's acknowledgements were eminently suitable to the occasion,
modest, grateful and dignified.

Then sprang up a friendly rivalry between the eminent
Alumni present, who should most gratefully express his sense
of the worth of their old Preceptor, and of his own personal
indebtedness to him. Other gentlemen also, some of whom
had been his associates in the duties of instruction, and some
who knew him only by his works, united with the Alumni in
bearing testimony to his excellences as a teacher and as a
man.

If *laudari a laudatis viris* be any compensation for a lifetime spent in the discharge of high and onerous duty, then
must Dr. Abbot have felt abundantly repaid for the pains he
had bestowed upon the generations who had been under his
tutelage, when he found himself the subject of so hearty,
sincere, discriminating eulogy from men of the character of
Edward Everett, Nicholas Emery, John G. Palfrey, George
Lunt, John P. Hale, Jonathan Chapman, Alexander H. Everett, Peter O. Thatcher, Gideon L. Soule, Henry Ware, Jr.,
Prentiss Mellen, Charles S. Daveis, Caleb Cushing, Ichabod
Nichols, and others who took part in these exercises.

But perhaps nothing that was said attracted more attention than the opening remarks of the venerable Judge Jeremiah Smith :—"I can claim a distinction which belongs to no
other man living. You were Dr. Abbot's scholars. I was
his teacher." "I then thought him, and have since found
him, exactly fitted for the station in which Providence placed

him." It was while Dr. Abbot was pursuing his preparatory
studies at Andover, that the speaker, then an assistant in the
Academy there, enjoyed the privilege of speeding on the
pathway of learning, the youth, who was now, after accomplishing his useful and meritorious life work, about to quit
the scene of his labors and his triumphs.

Three odes were composed for this occasion, and were
sung from printed copies, during the exercises, by the entire
company, with feeling and expression. One of them, which
was again sung, thirty-four years afterward, on a similar occasion, when the dedication of the new Academy building,
was substantially united with the Farewell to Dr. Gideon L.
Soule on his retirement from the Principal's chair, and may
therefore fairly be considered as *the* Academy Song, is here
given.*

SONG FOR THE ABBOT FESTIVAL.
BY REV. HENRY WARE, JR.
Tune, "Sandy and Jenny."

From highways and byways of manhood we come,
And gather, like children, about our old home;
We return from life's weariness, tumult and pain,
Rejoiced in our hearts to be schoolboys again.

The Senator comes from the hall of debate,
The Governor steps from the high chair of State,
The Judge leaves the bench to the law's wise delay,
Rejoiced to be schoolboys again for a day.

The Parson his pulpit has left unsupplied,
The Doctor has put his old sulky aside,
The Lawyer his client has turned from the door,
And all are at Exeter,—schoolboys once more.

Oh, glad to our eyes are these dear scenes displayed,
The halls where we studied, the fields where we played,

*For the other two odes, see Appendix II. One of them is said
to have been written by Mr. Abel F. Hildreth, an old pupil, and
long the respected head of the Pinkerton Academy in Derry, New
Hampshire. He was present on this occasion, and no doubt led
with his powerful and well trained voice, the singing of the several pieces.

There is change—there is change—but we will not deplore,
Enough that we feel ourselves schoolboys once more.

Enough that once more our old Master we meet,
The same as of yore when we sat at his feet,
Let us place on his brow every laurel we've won,
And show that each pupil is also a son.

And when to the harsh scenes of life we return,
Our hearts with the glow of this meeting shall burn;
Its calm light shall cheer till earth's schooltime is o'er,
And prepare us in Heaven for one meeting more.

In the evening Dr. Abbot's house was thrown open and crowded with ladies and gentlemen, anxious to pay him their respects; and a *soiree* was held at the Squamscott House. The ceremonies of the day were in every respect worthy of the extraordinary occasion, and afforded complete satisfaction to the friends of the Academy.

III.

THE ACADEMY; 1838 to 1883.

After Dr. Abbot's resignation was finally accepted, the Trustees unanimously made choice of Gideon L. Soule, A. M., Professor of Ancient Languages, as his successor. He had been for more than sixteen years an associate of Dr. Abbot in the corps of instructors, and by reason of the impaired health of the latter had practically exercised the powers of Principal for some time prior to his election. He was therefore perfectly familiar with the methods and the traditions of the institution, and no immediate changes in the administration, worthy of note, occurred on the transfer of authority from the old to the new head of the school.

The English department, which had been instituted as a distinct branch in 1808, was deemed, forty years afterward, to have diminished in importance. The number of academies and high schools in the country, where English studies could be conveniently pursued, had in that period greatly increased. For this reason, and because also in that division of the Academy "not one for the last seven years had completed the course of study prescribed," the English department, as a distinct feature of the school, was discontinued. This, however, was not construed to debar any individual members of the Academy who might choose to do so, from prosecuting a more complete course of study in the English branches than that included in the ordinary preparation for college.

It had always been the aim of the Trustees, from the opening of the Academy, to render the charitable aid provided by the Founder, of the highest possible utility to those who enjoyed it. In the earlier days, when the cost of the necessaries of life was small, the allowance made from the foundation to indigent students, was sufficient for their comfortable subsistence. But as the number of students increased, while fewer of the families resident in the town were willing to receive them as boarders, and the cost of living steadily advanced, it was at length found that the sum allotted to each beneficiary was wholly inadequate to his support. The Trustees, therefore, determined to establish at the charge of the Academy, a dormitory and commons hall for the members of the school of limited means, by which the expense of living should be reduced to the minimum. The experiment was first made in the building owned by the Academy on Spring street, which had formerly been the printing establishment of the Messrs. Williams. Here the rooms were rented for a merely nominal sum, and the board was furnished at the exact cost. The result of the experiment was so satisfactory that in 1852 the Trustees voted to erect a more suitable and capacious building for the same purpose, in the Academy grounds. It was completed and opened for use in 1855. It was constructed of brick, and contained rooms for fifty young men, with a dining hall and other needful accommodations; and cost about twenty thousand dollars. The name of Abbot Hall was appropriately given to it. The building has fully answered the uses for which it was designed. Every room in it has been constantly occupied, and the inmates have been enabled to live with entire comfort at about one-half the ordinary charges of the boarding houses.

The size and importance of the school, and the number of its instructors, seemed now to demand a more systematic administration; and it was thought expedient, in 1857, to invest the Principal, Professors and permanent instructors with the powers of a regular Faculty. This arrangement has ever

since been maintained, and has been found to conduce to
harmony, to uniformity in discipline, and to higher respect
for authority, in the school.

It was in the year 1857 that an application was made to
the Trustees to modify the regulations of the Academy so far
as to allow girls to be admitted as pupils. It is not known
whether the project met the approval of any members of the
board, for the petitioners, upon learning that it was strongly
objected to by some of them, thought proper to withdraw
the application.

The year 1858 witnessed a notable innovation in the
Academy. Up to that date the pupils had been required to
do the greater part of the preparation, as well as the recita-
tion, of their lessons in the school-rooms, which necessarily
confined them therein for five or six hours on every week
day, Wednesday and Saturday excepted, when the sessions
were abbreviated about one-half. Besides being irksome to
both teachers and pupils, this method was objectionable on
sanitary grounds; but probably another consideration had
much weight with the authorities of the Academy in induc-
ing them to change it.

The plan of keeping the pupils under constant sur-
veillance had never been practiced in this Academy. All
the liberty that was consistent with good discipline had always been granted them. They were treated as little like
children, and as nearly like men, as their conduct would war-
rant. The habit of self-reliance and self-government had
been so thoroughly inculcated by these practical lessons,
that the authorities felt justified in putting the students upon
the footing of those in more advanced institutions. Our
colleges and professional seminaries required the presence
of their students only at recitations and prayers, and per-
mitted them to pass the remainder of their time at their
rooms. In Phillips Academy, at Andover, the older part of
the pupils, at least, enjoyed the same privilege. It was not
doubted that equal freedom might be allowed all the students

of this Academy, without danger of abuse. The former rule was therefore relaxed, and "studying out of school," by young and old alike, was introduced. It has proved, to all concerned, teachers and learners alike, a great physical relief, and has operated in no way to the detriment of the school. The character and quantity of the work done under the new regime have fully equalled, if they have not exceeded, the former standard.

In the year 1859, Professor Joseph G. Hoyt, who had been connected with the Academy in the department of Mathematics for nearly eighteen years, resigned the position, to accept the office of Chancellor of the Washington University at St. Louis.

In the year 1862 the Rev. John Langdon Sibley, long the excellent Librarian of Harvard College, laid the foundations of a separate charity fund, which, by subsequent additions and stipulations, was to be allowed to accumulate, by adding the yearly interest to the principal, until it reached the amount of $100,000, after which the income was to be applied within certain restrictions, to the aid of students of the Academy, "of poverty and merit." The endowment was to be known by the name of the "Sibley Charity Fund," and was to be regarded as a memorial of the donor's father, Dr. Jonathan Sibley, a native of New Hampshire, and long a resident of Maine, from whose accumulations it was in part derived. He had always deeply sympathized with young men struggling to obtain an education, and was especially grateful to this Academy for the assistance which it furnished his son in his preparation for College. The Trustees accepted the gift with the stipulations annexed to it. The fund now amounts to about $34,000.

On the night of the seventeenth of December, 1870, the old Academy building, which was erected in 1794, and enlarged in 1821, was destroyed by fire. It had long been felt to be inconveniently small and unsuitable, for the increasing number of students; but its proportions were architecturally harmonious, and it was so associated in the minds of thousands of Alumni with the pleasant period of their school-days, that its disappearance, caused a pang in many a breast.

But not a moment's doubt rested in the minds of the friends of the Academy, of the readiness of grateful and philanthropic hearts to do more than make good the loss. Three days after the catastrophe, a committee of the Trustees published a statement of what was needed to enable the Academy to replace the former building with a new and more convenient one, and an appeal to the Alumni and friends of the school to contribute the means for the purpose. The call was promptly responded to, and immediate subscriptions enabled the committee to proceed with the work of rebuilding, without delay, and the whole needed amount of nearly $50,000 was seasonably obtained.*

The new building was completed in the early part of 1872. It was placed nearly on the spot where its predecessor for more than three-quarters of a century had stood. It was designedly made not unlike that, in its general outlines, but its material was brick, its dimensions were much enlarged and many improvements introduced. Altogether the new home of the school was far more elegant, commodious and suitable than the old.

By a general understanding, and without the expenditure of any special effort, the opening of the new edifice, erected by the munificence of those who loved and valued the Academy, was to be made a red-letter day in its calendar. The occasion in fact possessed a double interest, for it also commemorated the completion of the semi-centenary of Dr. Soule's continuous service in the Academy. The venerable second Principal had sought to be relieved of his charge at this time, but, at the instance of the Trustees, consented to

*Among the many noble contributions for this object, it is interesting to note that the largest one of $10,000, was from William Phillips, Esq., of Boston, a kinsman of the Founder.

hold his office, though freed from its more onerous duties, for a year longer.

The new Academy building was dedicated on the nineteenth day of June, 1872. The Trustees had designated the Rev. Dr. Andrew P. Peabody, President of the board, to deliver the dedicatory address ; and the gathering of Alumni, invited guests and others, to witness the ceremonies, was imposing. The exercises of the morning were held in the new and spacious Academy hall, which was thronged. A number of gentlemen of distinction were placed upon the stage, while portraits of the Founder and of other benefactors, trustees and teachers, gathered in great part by the exertions of one of the Alumni,* looked down from the walls. The Rev. Dr. John H. Morison opened the exercises with an appropriate prayer ; after which the Rev. Dr. Peabody delivered his admirable address, which is accessible in print, and needs no further notice here.

In the afternoon a procession was formed, and marched to the town hall, where the dinner was served. The Rev. Dr. Palfrey presided at the tables, and in due time invited the attention of the company to the intellectual part of the feast. He pronounced a merited encomium upon the wisdom and philanthropy of the Founder, and exhibited some interesting relics of him, which had been presented by his family. Announcing as the first sentiment, to be drunk in pure water, "the memory of the Founder," he called upon the oldest graduate present, the venerable John Swasey. of Bucksport, Maine, who made a happy response.

Wendell Phillips, the well known orator and reformer, was then introduced, amid acclamations. He said that his relationship to the Founder was so distant, that he could speak of his endowment of the Academy without a pang, and of his virtues as freely as if they adorned any other name. He adverted to Dr. Phillips' rigid economy in his personal

---

*The Hon. Benjamin F. Prescott, since Governor of New Hampshire.

expenses, and of his liberality to the clergy, which he illustrated by pertinent anecdotes. He applauded the example so early set by the Phillips family, of employing their wealth for the enlargement of the means of education ; but admired still more the faithfulness of the Trustees of the Academy who had accomplished so great results, not only without diminution of the fund, but while increasing it to twice its original dimensions. More is required of us, he said, than of our fathers, on account of our present opportunities ; we shall not do as well as they did, unless we surpass them. He lamented that the early fashion of uniting work with study was not still preserved. There is now too much book education and too little practical education. He lamented also, the timidity that prevailed among the educated men of America. They no longer lead the people, but are dragged along by the people. If the scholars of the country had done their duty, there would have been no civil war, with its enormous debt. He trusted that when the next victory shall be won for reform, the victor will not have it in his power to say to the American scholar, as Henry IV said to Crillon, after one of his great battles—"*tu n'y etais pas*"—"such a day as we had, and you not there !"

The next sentiment was in honor of the venerable Principal, Dr. Gideon L. Soule. His health at this time was so feeble as to have precluded him from attending the exercises of the morning, but he felt that he could not be absent from this fraternal festivity. He acknowledged, in a brief but felicitous speech, the honor conferred upon him, and then apologized for being compelled to withdraw. The entire company rose and saluted him with cheers as he retired from the hall.

President Paul A. Chadbourne being called upon, responded in a brief review of his school days at Exeter, in which he paid a high tribute to the influence of Dr. Soule as an instructor, and declared that the Latin lessons he had learned at the Academy he never could forget.

To a sentiment complimentary of the board of Trustees, the Hon. Amos Tuck, one of the oldest members, made a fitting response. He passed in review the work of the Academy during the years that he had been concerned in its government, and pointed with gratification to the improvements which had been introduced; instancing the thorough classification of students; the clothing of the permanent instructors with the powers of a Faculty, and the dispensing with the attendance of the pupils in the school rooms for the purposes of study.

The Hon. George S. Hale, the youngest in office of the Trustees, was then called on, and after giving some pleasant reminiscences of his student life, he concluded with an original poem, which is reserved for another place in this volume.*

Brief remarks were also offered by Prof. Francis Bowen, by the Hon. Jeremiah Smith, a Trustee and the son of the earlier Trustee of the same name; by the Rev. Dr. Roswell D. Hitchcock, of New York; and by Principal Tilton, of Phillips Andover Academy.

The Rev. John Langdon Sibley, who was now for the first time publicly announced as the donor of the generous fund, recently presented, for the aid of students of poverty and merit, was called to his feet. He modestly explained the motives which induced him thus to dispose of his patrimony, as well as to supplement it from his own earnings; and stated that it had been his design not to have his name known in the transaction, but it was found that the secret would not be kept, and he had yielded to the persuasion of friends of the Academy that the announcement should be made on this occasion. Mr. Sibley's statement was listened to with the deepest interest, and was one of the most touching incidents of the day.

The Song which had been composed by the Rev. Henry Ware for the Abbot Festival, and sung there thirty-four years

---

*Appendix 1.

before, was then executed by the company under the leadership of Mr. Sibley ; and the exercises were closed.

In the evening a promenade concert and dance at the town hall, brought the day to a happy termination.

In the year 1873, Dr. Soule, having now completed more than half a century's duties in the Academy, and having retained the office of Principal for the last year only because the Trustees "would not let him go," definitively resigned his position. In accepting his resignation, the Trustees voted,—"that the President be requested to express to, Dr. Soule the grateful sense entertained by the board, of the value of his long continued services, and to request him to accept the title of Principal Emeritus of Phillips Exeter Academy."

Albert Cornelius Perkins, A. M., was elected to fill the vacancy occasioned by Dr. Soule's resignation, and entered upon his duties at the beginning of the year 1873-74. He was a graduate of Dartmouth College in the class of 1859, and received from his *alma mater* the degree of Doctor of Philosophy in 1879.

There was found in the year 1873 a scarcity of suitable rooms in the town for the accommodation of the members of the Academy, who were yearly increasing in number. To meet this want the capacious brick building originally known as the Squamscott House was purchased by the Trustees, and fitted up as a lodging and boarding house for students. Its name was changed to "Gorham Hall," in memory of the late Dr. David W. Gorham, long a useful and respected member of the board of trust.

Several rooms in it are reserved for transient guests, with an eye especially to the convenience of relatives and friends of the boys attending the Academy.

In 1874 the capacity of the Academy to furnish help to students of restricted means, was much augmented by the bounty of Jeremiah Kingman, Esq., a gentlemen of property in Barrington, New Hampshire. By his will he constituted the Academy his residuary legatee; the income of the bequest to be applied annually to "the support of indigent meritorious students attending said Academy." From this source the sum of nearly $40,000 has been added to the resources of the Academy, which is termed the "Kingman Fund," and is kept separate from the general assets of the institution.

During the year following, Woodbridge Odlin, Esq., of Exeter, impressed with a conviction of the value, especially to the youth of his town, of an English course of instruction, offered to the Academy a donation of $20,000 for the purpose of founding a professorship of English in the school, to be known by his name. This of course implied the revival in the Academy of the English department, which had been for many years discontinued. There was some difference of opinion among the Trustees, with regard to the advisability of restoring a distinct branch of instruction, which had been found, on a former experiment, in a great measure to have lost its attractions for students; but on mature deliberation they decided to accept the generous proposal of Mr. Odlin, and the English department was reinstated.

In 1879 a friend of education, who desired that his name should not be publicly announced, completed a donation to the general fund of the Academy of ten thousand dollars; of which one-half had been forwarded two years previously. The presentation was accomplished through the medium of the Hon. Amos Tuck, a member of the board of trust.

In the succeeding year Henry Winkley, Esq., of Philadelphia, a gentleman well known by his generous contributions for worthy objects, sent to the Trustees his second gift of five thousand dollars,—making the sum of ten thousand dollars in all,—to be used "for the benefit and purposes of the Academy as they might think best."

This outline sketch of the rise and century's progress of

Phillips Exeter Academy would hardly be complete without
a picture of it as it is at the present time.

Externally it has undergone vast changes from its first
estate. The number of instructors has trebled ; that of the
pupils has quintupled. The one plain scanty building has
expanded into three, of imposing dimensions,—the Academy
proper, architecturally elegant, and furnished with every
desirable convenience, Abbot Hall and Gorham Hall, handsome and commodious houses for boarding and lodging a
hundred students. An ample yard around the main building, and a spacious "campus" a third of a mile distant, furnish abundant room for all out-door games and amusements.

The inside has changed no less than the outside. The
school which at first was scarcely superior to those in the
districts of a country town, has now become a seminary for
advanced, and specially thorough, instruction. It would be
hazarding little to say that the graduates of our highest institutions a hundred years ago, were not so accurately drilled
in their classics or their mathematics, as are the Exeter boys
who have gone through the course of preparation for admission to college to-day.

In fact the school has taken on many of the features of a
college. All the students belong to the regular yearly classes,
of which there are four in the classical, and three in the English department. They are designated in the college fashion
as Juniors, Seniors, &c., the title of the members of the preparatory class being characteristically abbreviated to "Preps."

The permanent members of the board of instruction are
organized into a Faculty, with the powers vested in such a
body by our colleges. They hold their regular weekly meetings, and after consideration and deliberation together, decide
all questions of discipline, &c.

All the pupils study in their own private rooms, and meet
in the school building only for prayers and recitations. The
fact that they are freed, while at their studies, from the irksome confinement of the school room, and are neither under

the eye of a teacher or a monitor, nor expected to repress
every sign of impatience of restraint, tends to give them a
stronger sense of independence and self-reliance. During
the hours assigned for study they are required to remain in
their own rooms; and punctuality in attendance at recitations and prayers, is of course insisted on.

Phillips Exeter Academy is not a reformatory; nor does
it profess to furnish attendants for feeble-minded youth. It
aims to make its pupils thorough and accurate scholars in
the branches which it teaches, to see that they are kept free
from evil influences, and to direct and encourage them to
virtuous and manly principles. No vicious lad, who is liable
to contaminate his associates, is allowed to remain an hour
in the school. The Halls and the boarding houses are under
the control of the Faculty, so that every instance of irregu-
lar or improper conduct therein is promptly reported to
them. Without hampering the boys with a thousand petty
restrictions, they are thus able to learn the character, the
habits, the needs and the dangers of each. If a boy lacks
the power of self-command to keep him from continually fall-
ing into serious harm, this is not the place for him. His
masters are ready to do much for him, but they cannot
act as corks for him to swim with. The youth who cannot,
or will not, keep fairly up with the studies of his class, must
either go back into a lower one, or migrate elsewhere.

But those young men or boys who are willing to make the
most of their powers, receive here every encouragement.
Their instructors feel and cultivate a personal interest in
every one of them. They consult with them freely, respecting their plans and difficulties, and are enabled by their
experience to give them valuable practical help. Numbers
of the prosperous men of our country regard the counsel, not
less than the instruction, which they received at the Academy, as the foundation of their success in life. Exeter prides
herself no less on the manly, than on the scholarly character
of the young men whom she has trained.

The beneficiary system of the Academy is administered upon a plan which is believed to combine the greatest practicable good, with the least admixture of evil. All pecuniary assistance to students is based upon the united considerations of restricted means, and merit in its widest signification. It is not intended merely to enable young men to enter the clerical profession, or any single line of usefulness; nor may it be claimed by all whose moral or religious character is immaculate. It is intended to operate as a reward and an encouragement to good principles and good conduct, diligence and scholarship, and is never conferred until the results of at least one term of study have shown the recipient's fitness; and is yearly re-adjusted, that it may be a continuing force..

The combined bounty of the Founder and of Mr. Kingman maintain twenty "foundation" scholarships, each yielding $60 per annum, or a little more than a dollar and a half a week during term-time. These are assigned to the most deserving pupils in all the four classes. There are also four special scholarships,—the gifts respectively of the Hon. George Bancroft, of the Rev. Dr. Charles Burroughs, of the Hon. Nathaniel Gordon, and of Miss Martha Hale, daughter of the Hon. Samuel Hale. They are known by the names of their several donors, and are of the yearly value of from $70 to $140 each. They are usually divided between the two higher classes. Free tuition is afforded to all the recipients of scholarships, as of course; and to about double the number of other students, whose circumstances are thought to require it. Abbot Hall contains accommodations for fifty boys, and the rent of rooms there, being trifling, and the price of board being adjusted to cover the mere cost, the maintenance of about one-fourth part of the whole school is thus reduced to the lowest rate of expense.

The problem how to make young men beneficiaries, without sapping the foundations of their manliness and self-respect, has never arisen here. There are no invidious distinctions drawn between the rich and the poor, either by the authorities, or what is more important, among the students themselves. Every advantage which is afforded by the school to one class, is open to all. And it is a fact, equally remarkable and honorable, that those who receive assistance from the funds of the Academy, are not even known by any distinctive name.

The record shows that a very large proportion of the distinguished men who have studied in the Academy were beneficiaries. And as Exeter owes so much of her celebrity to her charity-scholars of the past, she is never likely to undervalue those of the present.

In its religious character, Phillips Exeter Academy is completely unsectarian. The directions of the Founder concerning the orthodoxy of the Principal, and the Protestanism of the Trustees and instructors, have been implicitly obeyed, and his personal example of tolerance of theological differences has not been overlooked.*

The boys who attend the school have been bred in various forms of belief, and no attempt is made to proselyte them to any other. They are at liberty on Sundays to attend the church of whatever denomination they, or their guardians direct; but attendance on divine worship *somewhere*, is obligatory on all. Prayers and scripture reading are daily exercises of the school; and virtuous conduct and respect for the ordinances of religion are sedulously inculcated by the instructors, by precept and example.

---

*It is proper to state that though Dr. Abbot's theological views, in his later life, are admitted to have differed widely from those entertained by the Founder, and though it has been repeatedly affirmed that such was the case in the Founder's lifetime, yet the latter assertion has recently been denied.

IV.

THE INSTRUCTORS.

WILLIAM WOODBRIDGE, the first Preceptor of Phillips Exeter Academy, was a native of Glastonbury, Connecticut, and was born on the fourteenth of ·September, 1755. He was the son of the Rev. Ashbel Woodbridge, the minister of that town, and was the fifth in lineal descent from the Rev. John Woodbridge, who emigrated from England to this country. William Woodbridge graduated from Yale College in 1780, and elected teaching as his occupation, though he also qualified himself for the duties of a minister of the gospel.

It was probably through family relations who lived in the vicinity of Dr. Phillips, that Mr. ·Woodbridge became known to him. A cousin of the Rev. Ashbel Woodbridge was the wife of the Rev. John Clark, a former minister of the first parish in Exeter, and, after his decease, married the Rev. John Odlin his successor in the same charge. She was the mother of several children, whose homes were in and around Exeter.

The infirmity of Mr. Woodbridge's health, while he was the Preceptor of the Academy, did not suffer him fairly to show what he was capable of accomplishing. A new school, under an invalid master, could hardly be expected to thrive. Yet notwithstanding this serious check upon his capacity for useful exertion, the Trustees undoubtedly held his merits in high regard. The Resolution which they adopted, upon

accepting his resignation, may be relied on as the more sincere expression of their real sentiments, as it was passed
before commendations of parting officials had degenerated
into mere matters of course :

"Resolved, that the thanks of this board be given to Mr.
Woodbridge for his faithful services and unwearied exertions, while Preceptor of Phillips Exeter Academy, to instil
into the minds of the youth committed to his care, the principles of Piety and Virtue, as well as to instruct them in useful knowledge ; and as he has declared it inconsistent with
his health and sense of duty to continue longer in that rela-
tion to the Academy, this board wish him the high reward
of observing satisfactory fruits of his past labors, and that
his services, in whatever sphere he may hereafter move, may
be crowned with distinguished usefulness."

Mr. Woodbridge, after leaving Exeter, was associated
with his sister in the charge of an academy for young ladies
in Medford, Massachusetts, and followed his profession of
teaching through life, uniting with it from time to time the
functions of a preacher, also.

While living in Exeter he married Elizabeth, daughter of
Deacon Samuel Brooks. In his later years he contributed
articles for the "Annals of Education," of which his son
William C. Woodbridge, the well-known geographer, was
the editor. Though his health was feeble, yet he attained
great age, and died in Franklin, Connecticut, the twenty-
seventh of March, 1836, "an honored teacher of fifty years'
standing."

The successor of Mr. Woodbridge in the immediate charge
of the Academy, must have been known personally, as well
as by repute, to the Founder. He was a native of the same
town, and lived in the same parish, wherein the father of Dr.
Phillips was pastor for sixty years ; and was prepared for
college at the Academy in Andover of which the Doctor was
the chief benefactor and a punctual and observant Trustee.
We have the assurance, too, that it was at the immediate

request of the Founder that Mr. Abbot received his invitation to Exeter.

BENJAMIN ABBOT was the son of John Abbot, of Andover, Massachusetts, and was born there on the seventeenth of September, 1762. Five generations of the family had lived in the town; his father and grandfather were captains of the militia, when that office was a proof of courage and capacity; his lineal ancestors in the next two removes were both deacons of the church; all were resolute, pious men, of vigorous make, who lived long in the land.

Benjamin worked upon his father's farm until he was twenty years old, and then resolved to acquire a college education. He prosecuted the study of Latin at the infant Academy in his native town, where he became a pupil of Jeremiah Smith, then an assistant teacher there, with whom he was destined in after years to be associated in the board of control of the Academy in Exeter. He graduated from Harvard College in 1788, with high credit for his "scholarship and moral worth," and the Salutatory Oration was assigned him at Commencement. In the following August he entered upon his duties in Phillips Exeter Academy.

Nature had gifted him with qualities which singularly fitted him to be a tutor and governor of youth. The blood of his ancestors seems to have blended their several excellences in his veins. He was accustomed, in after years, to attribute his professional success to his observance of the rule, *suaviter in modo, fortiter in re;* which in his case might not unaptly be translated "deacons' words, captains' deeds." Though inflexibly just, he was only too happy to temper justice with mercy, whenever it would not be subversive of good discipline. He was never over ready to take notice of a fault that might be passed by without harmful consequences. It was a favorite remark of his that "it was a great accomplishment to know how to wink!" Probably many a boy attributed to his teacher's want of observation, what was really the result of merciful voluntary blindness.

Though he shrank from causing pain to the lowest creature, yet in those instances where punishment was really merited, he inflicted it without flinching. In the happily rare cases in which he had to deal with a vicious or depraved lad, he administered a lesson, both to mind and body, that served as a wholesome reminder of duty. He was not the man to spoil the child, in such cases, by sparing the rod. In general, however, he governed with the least possible display of authority. In the school-room, a look, a tap on the desk, or a shake of the forefinger was enough to recall the wandering attention of the most wayward, and fix it upon the business of the hour. But govern he did, and that most effectually. Modest and retiring as he was with regard to matters unconnected with his peculiar province, "no admiral on the quarter-deck of his flag-ship was, more than he in his school, the impersonation of decision, firmness and authority."*

From his first appearance at Exeter, he devoted himself wholly to his school. He is represented by those who knew him as a young man, to have been even then distinguished for maturity of judgment and power of command. He took no part in political affairs, or in neighborhood differences ; he had no ambitions beyond his chosen vocation. He set an example of industry and perseverence which could not fail to have lasting weight in the minds of his pupils. He studied the profession to which he devoted the long round of fifty years, with care and comprehension, and welcomed every substantial improvement in its methods. Not content with knowing the management of other academies, in our own country, he instituted particular inquiry into the conduct of the great English public schools, to which Exeter has been thought to be assimilated.

His scholastic acquirements were quite abreast of his time. No doubt the standard of scholarship was a different one at that day from what it now is. We are very much in fault if with all that modern research and criticism have done for us,

*The Rev. Dr. Morison.

we have not reached a higher level. Dr. Abbot was undoubtedly as learned and accurate a scholar in his age, as are the best of our educators in ours. An authentic anecdote gives an idea both of his philological attainments and of his impressive style of imparting information. One of his best pupils, John P. Robinson,* presented him his exercise in writing Latin, one day, for correction. Dr. Abbot returned it, with a single word marked as erroneous. Robinson consulted grammar and lexicon, and racked his brains to find out the mistake he had committed, but all in vain; and was at last obliged to take back the exercise to the Doctor, with the confession that he could not discover in what the fault lay. "Robinson," replied the Doctor, "words are like men; none but gentlemen are found in gentlemen's company." The difficulty was solved; and the pupil probably never afterwards forgot what was due to classical Latinity.

Dr. Abbot's moral influence over his disciples was the very best. He had a simple reverence for all that was good, and a transparent honesty of soul, which none about him could fail to remark and to respect. It took a bold, bad boy to attempt to deceive or to wrong him. All others felt that the Doctor was so genuinely good that it was a shame to take any advantage of him. And he, in his turn, treated his pupils with all possible courtesy, kindness and confidence.

He ruled by love rather than by fear. He had the art of getting very close to the boys, and without any surrender of dignity; near, yet afar. When he administered a reprimand, it never rankled. Every lad, not absolutely incorrigible, felt that he had a friend in "the Doctor."

His manners were such as would become a nobleman. Courteous as he was dignified, he doffed his hat in response to the greeting of the lowliest person he met. As he walked down the aisle of the school-room, bowing graciously to the

*The same who was afterwards satirized by Lowell, in the "Bigelow papers:"

"John P
Robinson he," etc.

right and left, his appearance so impressed every pupil, that the memory of it will never fade away. It made generations more mannerly.

Dr. Abbot was twice married. His first wife was Hannah Tracy Emery, of Exeter, who lived but two years after their marriage. Their only child was John Emery Abbot, who graduated from Bowdoin College, studied divinity, and was ordained the minister of the North church in Salem, Massachusetts. He died, deeply lamented, in 1819.

Dr. Abbot's second wife was Mary Perkins, of Boston, who survived him several years. Their children were Elizabeth, who married Dr. David W. Gorham, of Exeter, and Charles B. Abbot who resided in Glenburn, Maine. Dr. Gorham was for a long period one of the board of Trustees of the Academy, and after his decease his son Dr. William H. Gorham served for a time in the same capacity.

Dr. Abbot's life was prolonged until the twenty-fifth of October, 1849, when at the age of eighty-seven years, he was gathered to his fathers.

GIDEON LANE SOULE, the second Principal, was born in Freeport, Maine, the twenty-fifth of July, 1796. He entered the Academy in 1813, and after remaining three years, was admitted to the junior class of Bowdoin College, where he graduated in 1818. He then became an assistant teacher in the Academy for above a year, after which he entered upon a course of professional study,—but in the year 1822 he returned hither as a member of the corps of instructors, was subsequently appointed Professor of Ancient Languages, and on the withdrawal of Dr. Abbot in 1838, Principal of the Academy. Harvard College conferred upon him the honorary degree of Doctor of Laws, in 1856.

Dr. Soule had the advantage of a fine person ; he was tall, perfectly erect, and his air was dignified and commanding. His features were bold and handsome, his voice well modulated, his smile winning. His temper was equable, and his self-control was rarely disturbed.

Like Dr. Abbot, he possessed peculiar qualifications for
the position of chief of a great school. Many of his predecessor's methods he carried along into his own practice,
though his cooler temperament caused, perhaps, a more per-
ceptible distance between him and his pupils. But he understood well how to appeal to their better and nobler instincts,
and had confidence in their general rectitude of intention.
He never lost consciousness of the fact that boys were men
in miniature; and, looking forward through their present to
their future, always made a point of treating them in manly
fashion. He had a remarkable store of anecdotes, from
which he used to draw illustrations to enforce his teachings.
Here he never missed his aim. His happy allusions and
scholarly, clean cut sentences sent home to the understanding of the densest and least attentive of his flock, many a
wholesome truth that outlasted the memory of Latin and
Greek, in its salutary influence upon the life and character.

Dr. Soule was probably conservative by nature; he was
certainly so by position, for that necessarily comes of the
responsibilities attending authority. Yet his experience in
dealing with youth, and his recognition of the advance of
ideas in successive generations, induced him to countenance
changes which might have alarmed a more timid pilot. Under his administration the students made a great forward
stride in self-government. They were given to understand
that they were not to be held amenable to any written code,
but were to conform their conduct to the common law of
right and propriety, recognized by every member of an
enlightened community. And it was while he held the reins
of government, that the radical innovation of allowing all
the students the privilege of preparing lessons in their own
rooms, unwatched by tutors' eyes, was introduced. Notwithstanding the amount of freedom that had always been
allowed the members of the school, there is no doubt that
this experiment caused some anxiety. No doubt, too, the
Principal was somewhat influenced in his course by the

younger and more adventurous spirits that were his coadju-
tors in the Academy. But it argues well for his clear vision
and for his capacity for progress, that he yielded his concurrence in novelties, which successful experiment has demon-
strated to be improvements. Time has fully justified the
forward steps which he sanctioned, and the greater liberty
accorded the students has awakened a response, in the
increase of manliness and self-respect in the school.

As an instructor, especially in his chosen department, the
ancient classics, Dr. Soule's qualifications and success were
of the highest. In the Latin language and literature, to
which he gave special attention, he was pre-eminent. His
thorough knowledge, his critical exactness, his cultivated
taste, enabled him to make the study of the authors of anti-
quity a pleasure, instead of a task, to his pupils. "In this
department," it has been justly said, "he left his brilliant
record in all our colleges." No better work, no more thorough training presented itself for examination from any
quarter, than that which was accomplished under his immediate inspection.

It was a crucial test of Dr. Soule's capacity, that he was
chosen to follow Dr. Abbot, whose success had been so unex-
ampled, and who was regarded with such deference, not to
say reverence, by the community. A man of inferior parts
would have been dwarfed by the comparison. But the two
men had certain important qualities in common ; scholarship,
the gift of command, and especially that fine influence which
springs from innate courtesy and sense of justice. Both were
gentlemen, not merely in their manners, but in their hearts.
They set the example by words and acts, of Christian kindness and honorable sentiments, united with perfect urbanity.
They inspired their pupils not only with the love of learning,
but with an appreciation of the graces of character and of
the amenities of refined life.

It is the unanimous verdict that Dr. Soule wielded with
equal vigor and success, and that too, over a widening field,

the authority which his predecessor had employed to such
excellent purpose. Heartily and justly as the pupils of the
earlier Principal acknowledged their obligations to him for
his agency in developing whatever was best in their nature,
those who studied under his successor recognize the value of
his services and influence with no less gratitude and fervor.
To both is the Academy indebted, in equal measure, for its
past glories and its present efficiency.

Dr. Soule married Elizabeth Phillips Emery, of Exeter,
who survived him, to the age of more than eighty-eight years.
They had three children who reached adult age : Charles
Emery Soule, Assistant Surrogate in New York city ; Nicholas Emery Soule, who studied the profession of medicine,
but afterwards was the teacher of a classical school in Cin-
cinnati, Ohio ; and Augustus Lord Soule, formerly a Justice
of the Supreme Court of Massachusetts and now counsel of
the Boston and Albany Railroad corporation in Boston. Dr.
N. E. Soule has for several years been a Trustee of the
Academy.

Dr. Soule died in Exeter on the twenty-eighth of May,
1879. In view of the event, the Trustees adopted the following Resolution :

"Resolved, That the Trustees place upon the record some
expression of their regard for the character of the deceased,
and for the services he rendered to the Academy. His devotion to the interests of the school was unwavering. He
brought to the work of instruction and government, earnest
zeal, fine literary culture, love for young men, a nice sense
of honor and integrity, dignity and courtesy of a high order,
fidelity and generosity. These traits he applied with wisdom
and success to the interests of the young men under his care.
His love for the Academy and his concern for the welfare of
it ended only with his life. His name is cherished with affectionate veneration, and the reputation which the school acquired under his management is his fitting monument. The
Trustees desire to express their sympathy with the widow

and family of the deceased, and to join them in loving respect for his memory."

On the eighth of June following, the Rev. Dr. John H. Morison delivered, in the second church in Exeter, a discourse, commemorative of the excellent qualities and services of Dr. Soule, which was published at the expense of the Academy.

HOSEA HILDRETH, who was the second Professor of Mathematics and natural Philosophy in the Academy, and held that post from 1811 to 1825, deserves more than a passing notice. He was one of ten children of Timothy Hildreth, and was born in Chelmsford, Massachusetts, in the year 1782. Like not a few other men who have risen to distinction, his course in life was marked out for him by an accident. In his youth he received an injury to one of his arms, which by disqualifying him for manual labor, turned his attention to study. He graduated from Harvard College in 1805, and prepared himself for the ministry, and, it is said, was always fonder of preaching than of teaching. In addition to his work of instruction in the Academy he supplied the pulpit of the second parish in Exeter from 1813 to 1817, when the Rev. Isaac Hurd was installed there. And when he quitted the Academy, in 1825, it was to assume the charge of a religious society in Gloucester, Massachusetts.

Professor Hildreth's influence in the school was very positive and very salutary. He possessed decided traits of character; strong convictions and a resolute will, united with much learning and ready wit. He was the projector of the Golden Branch Society, which, under his administration, no doubt acted as a keen stimulus to study and to the desire for improvement. His countenance bore the impress of his originality and humor, so that the eccentric Robert Treat Paine declared that it might be "cut up into a thousand epigrams."

After officiating for about eight years as the minister of Gloucester, Mr. Hildreth took the office of Secretary of the Massachusetts Temperance Society, which he filled with efficiency and zeal, and ended his useful life at Stirling, Massachusetts, the tenth of July, 1835. He was the author of several productions of merit ; among them of "a Book for New Hampshire Children," which for a number of years held its place in the schools of the State, as a juvenile text-book, and passed through several editions.

Professor Hildreth married Sarah McLeod, of Boston, who survived him more than thirteen years. They had seven children, of whom the three sons, Richard, Samuel T., and Charles H. Hildreth were all members of the Academy. The eldest of these was the distinguished editor and historian. None of them is now living except the youngest son, Dr. Charles H. Hildreth, of Gloucester, Massachusetts.

JOSEPH GIBSON HOYT, who filled the chair of Mathematics in the Academy for nearly eighteen years, was born in Dunbarton, New Hampshire, on the nineteenth of January, 1815. His father was a plain farmer ; but his mother was a gifted and ambitious woman. Until he was sixteen years old, he was employed upon his father's farm, so that he was unable to attend school more than three months in the year. But before he was eighteen he began to study with a view to a collegiate education. For five winters he taught country schools to obtain the means to carry out his design. He entered Yale College in 1836, and graduated with high credit in 1840. He was then employed as a preceptor for a year ; and in 1841 was called to Phillips Exeter Academy. While here he gave instruction in Greek, as well as in his own special branches ; and in all showed himself possessed of much learning, originality and genius. He was full of fire and enthusiasm, and had the art of inspiring his pupils with no little of the same. Not content with performing his academical duties, he manifested a deep interest in everything that was transpiring around him, and in the great world. He was a reformer, and a politician. In 1850 he was chosen a member of the Convention called to revise the Constitution of New Hampshire ; and in 1858 he became an aspirant for

Congressional honors, but failed of the nomination, by a
narrow margin. He was enthusiastic in every scheme of
improvement in the town of his residence. 'For some years
he was a member of the Superintending School Committee,
and his reports upon the condition of some of the schools in
the outlying districts, brimming over with his quaint humor,
are racy reading to-day.

The ardor of Professor Hoyt's temperament, while it gave
him efficiency and readiness, perhaps detracted somewhat from
the soundness of his judgment. He could occupy no conservative ground; he must be in the advance or nowhere, in
every movement. He had little patience with the caution
which felt its way before moving; and had no dread of
innovations. But in later years, after he had taken upon
himself the responsibility of a great educational institution,
there is reason to believe that he realized more than ever
before, the security that resides in a discreet conservatism.
Had his life been protracted, he would probably have carried on the development of the great work which he assumed,
with undiminished force, but with the circumspection gained
by experience.

In December, 1858, he accepted an invitation to the Chan-
cellorship of Washington University at St. Louis, Missouri,
and entered upon its duties at the beginning of the next
year. In July, 1859, Dartmouth College honored him with
the degree of Doctor of Laws. He had occupied his new
position for scarcely two years, before his health began to
give way. He tried every means to regain it, but without
success, and at length on the twenty-sixth of November,
1862, he sank into the grave.

Professor Hoyt married Margaret Chamberlain, of Exeter,
who, together with four, it is believed, of their five children.
is still living.

In selecting the foregoing from the roll of instructors for
special notice, because they have occupied the prominent
positions, and have been longest connected with the man-

agement of the Academy, there is no disposition to under-
rate the value of the services of others, of character and
accomplishments scarcely if at all inferior, who have also
exerted their full share of influence in shaping the course,
and adding to the celebrity of the school.   It is doubtful if
any institution in the land can boast so extraordinary a suc-
cession of teachers. as Exeter has enjoyed.   Year after year,
the most brilliant and promising young men of their time,
after taking high honors at College, seem, as a matter of
course to have put their talents and their scholarship at the
disposal of Exeter.*

Daniel Dana, Nathan Hale, Alexander H. Everett.
Nathaniel A. Haven, Jr., Nathan Lord, Henry Ware, James
Walker, Joseph Hale Abbot, Theodore Tebbets, not to
mention others of the distinguished dead or of the distinguished living, were men of high mark, and exerted a power
for good in the Academy.   Indeed it is cause for much con-
gratulation and thankfulness, that this institution, founded
in the pure spirit of charity and philanthropy, has so wonder-
fully escaped the dangers of misrule and no rule, throughout
its life of a century, and has been so uniformly fortunate in
the selection of those to whom its authority and its work
have been delegated.

The present board of instruction consists of the following
members :

ALBERT C. PERKINS Ph. D. Principal, and Odlin Professor
of English.   Dr. Perkins is a native of Topsfield, Massachusetts, and a graduate of Dartmouth College.   Before coming
to Exeter he was an instructor in the Phillips Andover Academy, and in the Danvers High school ; and for ten years Master of the Oliver High school in Lawrence, Massachusetts.
He has resigned his post of Principal, and at the close of the
present school year will take the charge of the Adelphi Insti-
tute in Brooklyn, New York.

GEORGE A. WENTWORTH, A. M. Professor of Mathemat-

_____
*For a list of Instructors see Appendix J.

ies. Professor Wentworth is a native of·Wakefield, New Hampshire, and a graduate of Harvard College ; and has now been connected with the corps of instruction in the Academy for twenty-five years. He is the author of several text books in Mathematics, which have been extensively introduced in the higher seminaries of the country.

BRADBURY L. CILLEY, A. M. Professor of Ancient Languages. Professor Cilley was born and bred in Exeter, and graduated from Harvard College in 1859. Ever since that time he has been an instructor in the Academy. His special attention of late years has been given to the Greek language and Literature.

OSCAR FAULHABER Ph. D. Instructor in French and in German.

JAMES ARTHUR TUFTS A. B. Instructor in Latin and in English.

GEORGE LYMAN KITTREDGE, A. B. Instructor.

V.

The Officers, Benefactors and Alumni.

Of the many able and public-spirited men who, in various ways, have lent their aid to elevate the Academy to its present dignity, the limits of this sketch will admit only of concise notices of a few. The number of Trustees, in a century, has not exceeded forty, and their terms of office have averaged more than seventeen years each. Their services have of course been uncompensated, except by the satisfaction derived from witnessing the growing usefulness of the institution under their care. The fidelity of their conduct, in managing the pecuniary resources of the Academy, has been the subject of just encomium.

Oliver Peabody, an early and deeply interested member of the board, was the son of a farmer, and was born in Andover, Massachusetts, the cradle of so many of the early friends of the Academy, on the second of September, 1753. At the age of twenty he took his bachelor's degree at Harvard College; and, having completed the study of the law in the office of the Hon. Theophilus Parsons in Newburyport, Massachusetts, he established himself in Exeter, about the year 1781.

He soon rose into prominence. The year 1789 saw him Solicitor for the County; and the next year, State Senator and Judge of Probate. In 1793 and 1794 he sat again in the Senate, the latter year as President thereof. He then filled the office of Treasurer of the State for nine years. In

1805 he received the appointment of Sheriff of the County
for five years; and in 1813 he was again President of the
Senate. The same year he was commissioned a Justice of
the Court of Common Pleas; and remained upon the bench
until 1816. Three times he was chosen an Elector of President of the United States.

Judge Peabody, in addition to natural powers of a high
order, possessed the learning and cultivation which fitted him
to discharge the duties of the many important stations to
which he was preferred, with dignity and credit. Though
an excellent lawyer, he had no liking for contention, and was
seldom concerned in litigated causes in the Courts. Nature
formed him for popularity. Handsome in person, graceful
in manner, with a mild temper and a social disposition, he
won the confidence and good will of all. He took great
pleasure in society, and was the father of an interesting and
accomplished family. William B. O., and Oliver W. B.
Peabody, his twin sons, were students, and afterwards teachers, in the Academy; his only daughter was the wife of
Alexander H. Everett.

Judge Peabody was chosen a Trustee in 1794 and continued in the board for thirty-four years, the last twenty-two
of which he was also the Treasurer.

He died in Exeter, on the third of August, 1831.

JOHN TAYLOR GILMAN was born in Exeter, the nineteenth
day of December, 1753; received a common school education, and was bred to commerce and trade. On the morning
after the outbreak of hostilities at Lexington, he marched as
orderly sergeant of a company of active Whigs, to Cambridge, to render aid to the cause of his country. He did
not long remain in the field, for his services were needed
for the performance of equally patriotic duties at home. His
father, Col. Nicholas Gilman, the Treasurer of New Hampshire, was one of the most trusted and influential supporters
of the Revolution, and required the assistance of his efficient
son in providing the needful means to enable the State to

meet the exhausting calls that were made upon her for men and money. In the last two years of the Revolution the son was a delegate to the Continental Congress,—the youngest, but not the least influential member. In the year 1794 he was chosen to the office of Governor of New Hampshire, and his administration was so generally acceptable that he was retained in the position by successive re-elections until 1805. Again in 1813 he was recalled to the executive chair, and served for three years more, so that he held the office of Governor no less than fourteen years in all.

Gov. Gilman's patriotism and honesty were above question, even by his political opponents, and his capacity for business is proved by his constant employment in public affairs. He was appointed by Dr. Phillips to succeed him as Trustee, and occupied the position, greatly to the advantage of the Academy, from 1795 to 1827, when, on the ground of advanced years, he resigned it. By virtue of the privilege reserved by the Founder to himself and his appointee, Gov. Gilman might, if he had thought it expedient, have designated the person to succeed him in the trust ; but in a written communication, characterized by his usual sound sense and judgment, he declined to exercise the power. Gov. Gilman was President of the board from 1796 to the time of his resignation ; and Treasurer of the Academy from 1793 to 1806.

He was deeply interested in the welfare of the institution, and spared no time nor effort in its behalf. During the thirteen years that he acted as Treasurer, he refused all compensation for the service ; and in 1794, when it was determined to erect a new school building, he generously presented to the Academy two and a quarter acres of land, in a most eligible part of the town, as the site for it.

Of his four daughters the eldest married Nicholas Emery, an early instructor in the Academy, who became afterwards a Judge of the Supreme Court of Maine.

Gov. Gilman died in Exeter, August thirty-first, 1828.

DANIEL DANA was born in Ipswich, Massachusetts, the twenty-fourth of July, 1771. He graduated from Dartmouth College in the class of 1786, and was employed as an instructor in the Academy for about three years. He then studied divinity, and was settled as a minister, successively in Newburyport, Massachusetts, and in Londonderry, New Hampshire ; and afterwards over another parish in Newburyport. In the years 1820 and 1821 he occupied the office of President of Dartmouth College. As a preacher, a theologian and a ripe and thorough scholar, he deservedly maintained a high reputation.

Dr. Dana was chosen a Trustee of the Academy in 1809, and for thirty-four years discharged his duties with regularity and fidelity. He regarded the Academy as a nursery of learning and virtue, which demanded his utmost care and solicitude. The records of the Trustees bear abundant testimony to his willing and useful labors to promote its interests. His well-spent life was brought to a close, the twenty-sixth of August, 1859.

JEREMIAH SMITH was a native of Peterborough, New Hampshire, born the twenty-ninth of November, 1759. He entered Harvard College, but after a brief stay there, volunteered as a soldier in the Bennington campaign, where he received a wound. He completed his collegiate course at Rutgers College, in New Jersey, in 1780 ; then studied law, and was soon hailed as a rising man. He made his mark in the Legislature and in the Constitutional Convention of his native State in 1791-92, and afterwards in the Congress of the United States, where he sat for the term of six years. His abilities were recognized by his appointment to other offices of honor and responsibility by the Executive of the Nation and of the State, but it was probably as Chief Justice of the Superior Court of New Hampshire that he was most distinguished. He held the office from 1802 to 1809, when he resigned it on account of impaired health, and again from 1813 to 1816, when a reorganization of the Courts took place. In the interval between his two terms of judicial service, he was elected for a year as Governor of the State.

About 1820 Judge Smith retired from active business. His life was prolonged more than twenty years afterwards, however, and his powers of mind were never dimmed. He continued, until within a year or two of his death, to occupy his beautiful mansion on the western skirt of the village of Exeter, surrounded by his family and friends, universally respected, interested in affairs, enjoying his books, in a green and happy old age.

He was chosen to succeed Gov. Gilman as a Trustee in 1828, and was made President of the board in 1830. He resigned the position in 1842, when by reason of his removal from Exeter, and of bodily infirmity, he felt himself incapacitated for the performance of further duty. He also filled the office of Treasurer during the same period. His services to the Academy in various ways were of the greatest value. Through his encouragement many young men of promise were enabled to partake of the advantages of the school, of whom some became distinguished. His professional knowledge and his wise counsels were always a shield of safety to the institution.

Judge Smith died in Dover, New Hampshire, the twenty-first of September, 1842. His son, of the same name, was afterwards, for some years, a Trustee.

SAMUEL HALE was born in Barrington, New Hampshire, in the year 1793. His grandfather was the famous Major Hale, long master of the Grammar school in Portsmouth, and his father was a Judge of the Court of Common Pleas. He graduated from Bowdoin College in 1814, and began the study of divinity at the Theological School in Cambridge, Massachusetts. But his health being found too uncertain to admit of his undertaking pastoral duties, he was advised to adopt more active employment. For a time he resided in his native place, from which his fellow citizens elected him their Representative in the Legislature ; and afterwards he removed to Portsmouth, where he engaged in mercantile business. About the year 1842 he fixed his residence in Rollinsford, New Hampshire, and there passed the residue of his life, as a manufacturer.

Mr. Hale inherited an active temperament, and a love for letters. He is described by one of his associates in the board of trust* as "a man of singular vigor and energy, wise in counsel, prompt in action, of liberal culture and literary tastes ; and though always crowded with business of his own, always ready to give his time and best thought to the interests of learning."

He was chosen a Trustee in the year 1831 ; and in 1868 was promoted to the presidency of the board ; a position from which he was removed by death in December, 1869.

The Hale scholarship was established by the liberality of his daughter, Miss Martha Hale.

CHARLES BURROUGHS, born in Boston, Massachusetts, the twenty-seventh of December, 1787, was a graduate of Harvard College in the class of 1808, and, as a minister of the Protestant Episcopal denomination, was rector of St. John's church in Portsmouth, New Hampshire, for nearly fifty years. He was long identified with several benevolent and literary institutions, by his gifts thereto, and his services in their management.

Receiving his election to the board of Trustees of the Academy in 1835, he was chosen President of the same in 1844, and continued in that capacity until his death in 1867. A courteous gentleman, an accomplished scholar, filled with the spirit of kindness and humanity, he was specially drawn towards this fountain of learning, and as has been aptly said, held it "as second in his affections only to the church of which he was for more than half a century a loyal presbyter."

Dr. Burroughs by his will bequeathed to the Academy as a last testimony of his regard, the sum of $1,000, for the

---

*The Rev. Dr. Peabody.

foundation of the scholarship which is known by his name.

DAVID W. GORHAM, was a native of Canandaigua, New York, and was born in the closing year of the last century. At the age of fifteen he was admitted to the Academy, and in 1817 he entered Harvard College, graduating in due course in 1821. He studied the profession of medicine, and took up his residence in Exeter. He was naturally drawn more closely to the Academy, from the fact that he became the son-in-law of Dr. Abbot. He was elected a Trustee in 1844, and remained in the board until his decease in 1873; being succeeded therein by his son, Dr. William H. Gorham.

Dr. Gorham was remarkable for methodical business habits and sound discretion; qualities which were of essential value, in his connection with this trust. His advice was much relied upon by his associates, in all matters relating to the school, and he cheerfully gave his personal supervision to a great number of details that needed a constant and watchful eye.

The venerable widow of the first Principal, as long as she survived him, resided with her daughter in the family of Dr. Gorham.

AMOS TUCK was a native of Parsonsfield, Maine, born the second day of August, 1810. He lived on his father's farm until he was seventeen, and then prepared himself for college. Graduating from Dartmouth in 1835, he chose the profession of the law, and in 1838 began the practice in Exeter, in company with the Hon. James Bell, who was for some time a member of the board of Trustees. Their professional business for many years was one of the largest in the State. Mr. Tuck soon became interested in political matters. He was one of the leaders in the revolt against the democratic party, inaugurated by the Hon. John P. Hale, (a distinguished Alumnus of the Academy,) and, after having served in the State Legislature, was, in 1846, chosen a Representative in the Congress of the United States. He retained his seat, by successive re-elections, for six years.

Mr. Tuck was a prominent member of the "Peace Con-Congress," assembled in 1861, to devise measures, if possible, to avert the war. President Lincoln, who had been a fellow member of Congress with him, upon his accession to office, gave Mr. Tuck the appointment of Naval Officer at Boston, and upon the expiration of his commission in 1865, re-appointed him.

Mr. Tuck came into the board of Trustees in 1853, and continued there during the remainder of his life. He was a devoted friend of the Academy, and freely gave it the benefit of his legal knowledge and of his wide business experience. He was always interested in the subject of education, and had seen much service as a member of boards of trust of other institutions, so that his counsel and assistance were of peculiar value. This was so well understood that he was placed upon every committee of importance, with scarce an exception, during the period of his connection with the Academy. And it was through his intervention, that the gift of $10,000 was made to the general fund, by a friend, whose name is withheld from publication by his own desire.

Mr. Tuck died on the eleventh of December, 1879, at Exeter. The Trustees, in passing the Resolution customary on the decease of an associate, recited the many and varied ways in which he had rendered efficient service to the Academy, and concluded with the emphatic assertion,—"His name is among the foremost to be transmitted in our records, as friends and benefactors of the institution under our charge."

Other names upon the roll of the Trustees, both of the living, and of those whose earthly work is over, might fairly claim a place in these pages, did space permit.* But it seems proper not to dismiss the officers of the Academy, without at least a brief mention of some of those, not Trustees, who have had the immediate care of the fiscal concerns of the institution.

*For a list of the Officers see Appendix J.

JOHN KELLY was the son of the Rev. William Kelly, and was born in Warner, New Hampshire, the seventh day of March, 1786. At the age of eighteen he graduated from Dartmouth College, and adopted the profession of law. He was admitted to practice in 1808, and opened his office in Northwood, whose citizens soon after elected him as their Representative in the State Legislature. In 1814 he had a year's experience as editor of the Concord "Gazette," a newspaper printed at the capital of New Hampshire. He removed in 1831 to Exeter, on being appointed to the office of Register of Probate, which he held until 1842. In 1846 and 1847 he was a member of the Executive Council of the State.

Mr. Kelly always manifested a strong inclination for literature, and for historical study. After his removal to Exeter he took the editorial charge of the "News-Letter," and rendered the paper both entertaining and instructive. He possessed a fund of quaint humor, with which he enlivened the dryest subjects. A series of historical articles, respecting the early persons and events of New Hampshire, which Mr. Kelly published in the columns of his newspaper, were of peculiar value, and evinced in a remarkable degree his wide acquaintance with the subject, and his power of investing it with interest and attractiveness.

Mr. Kelly acted as the Treasurer of the Academy from 1842 to 1855. He died on the third of November, 1860.

Bradbury L. Cilley, A. M., Professor of Ancient Languages, and for the past twenty-four years an instructor in the Academy, is a grandson of Mr. Kelly.

JOSEPH TAYLOR GILMAN, a son of Col. Nathaniel Gilman, of Exeter, was born on the twelfth of October, 1811. He entered the Academy in 1822, and remained there for several years, until his school education was completed. He then became a clerk in his brother's store, and in 1835 sailed for China, and on arriving at Canton was taken into the employ of the important mercantile house of Russell & Co. There he remained, for a time as clerk, and afterwards as a partner, until the year 1846, when he retired from the firm with a competency, and returned tó his early home.

Here he passed the residue of his life, in the house where he was born; interested in the cultivation of his extensive farm, and in all that went on about him. His amiable disposition, kindness and courtesy secured him the regard of all who knew him, and his knowledge of character, sagacity and exact habits of business, rendered his co-operation sought for, in many important enterprises.

He assumed the Treasurership of the Academy in the year 1855, and performed the duties until within a few months of his decease, which occured in 1862. In accepting Mr. Gilman's resignation the Trustees requested the President to assure him of their high appreciation of "the good judgment, fidelity, accurate business habits and courtesy which he had manifested during the whole term of his office as Treasurer."

S. Clark Buzell was a native of Northwood, New Hampshire, and was born the eleventh of June, 1806. At the age of thirteen he was admitted to the Academy, and when he had reached nineteen, was engaged in a mercantile house in Boston, where he remained eleven years. He then returned to his native town, but removed in 1852 to Exeter, and resided there the remainder of his life. He received the appointment of Treasurer of the Academy in 1862, and resigned the office after having filled it for eighteen years.

He was methodical in his habits, and prudent and faithful in a remarkable degree. The Trustees, on his withdrawal from office, passed a resolution that "the President express to Mr. Buzell their thanks for his services, and a sense of their great value."

The first gift of money to the Academy, after the death of the Founder, was a legacy from the Hon. Nicholas Gilman, of $1,000, the income of which was to be applied to the instruction of students in vocal music.

Nicholas Gilman was a brother of Gov. John Taylor

Gilman, born in Exeter, the third of August, 1755. On attaining his majority he entered the army, and served through the Revolutionary war, the latter portion of the time as Assistant Adjutant General. In this capacity he took the account of the British prisoners on the surrender of Cornwallis at Yorktown.

Col. Gilman was long in public office. He was a delegate to the Continental Congress from 1786 to 1788, and a member of the Convention which framed the Constitution of the United States; a Representative in Congress from 1789 to 1797, and a Senator of the United States from 1805 to his death in 1814. His person was handsome, his manners were polished, and he possessed many accomplishments.

JEREMIAH KINGMAN, one of the principal benefactors of the Academy, was a native and life-long resident of Barrington, New Hampshire, where he died in 1872, at the advanced age of about eighty years. He was by occupation a farmer, a man of good natural ability, and of more than average education. In his later years he read much, and took more interest in books than in tilling the soil. In his younger days he represented his native town in the Legislature of the state.

He was interested in educational matters, and at one time supported a school in Barrington for those pupils who had advanced beyond the ordinary studies of the district schools. It is probable that his attention was specially directed to Phillips Exeter Academy by the successful career of his nephew, Professor Sylvester Waterhouse, (now of Washington University, St. Louis, Missouri,) who was a member of the Academy from 1847 to 1850.

JOHN LANGDON SIBLEY was born in Union, Maine, in 1804. He was fitted for college in the Academy, and completed his course at Harvard College in 1825. For two years after, he was assistant in the College Library, then studied for the profession of the ministry, and was ordained as pastor of the parish at Stow, Massachusetts, in 1829, but remained there only four years, when he returned to his old post in the College Library. In 1856 he was promoted to the position of chief librarian, which he continued to hold for about twenty years. He was a faithful and devoted officer, but found time to do no small amount of historical and literary work besides. He published in 1851 a history of his native town ; he was editor and proprietor of the "American Magazine of Useful and Entertaining Knowledge ;" he expended a large amount of labor upon the cataloguing of Harvard College, and has issued two capacious volumes of biographical records of the early graduates,—a marvel of patient and industrious research.

Mr. Sibley's father, a country physician and farmer, bequeathed him the sum of about five thousand dollars, the accumulations of a life of industry and frugality. This legacy the son preserved untouched, and presented it, a monument of filial affection, to the Academy by whose bounty he was provided with the means to pursue his studies. He largely added to it from his own means, so that now the aggregate has reached nearly seven times the amount of the original nucleus.

WOODBRIDGE ODLIN was an Exeter man by birth and by residence. His family was connected by marriage with that of Mr. Woodbridge, the first Preceptor of the Academy, and he doubtless owed his christian name to that circumstance. He acquired the chief part of his education at the Academy, having entered it at the age of twelve ; and he maintained his interest in it through life. Beginning his business career as a painter and manufacturer of carriages, he engaged subsequently in the wool trade, in which he became skilful and prosperous, and acquired a handsome fortune.

Mr. Odlin was a man of pronounced views. He had a ready speech and an impressive manner, and addressed public meetings with much effect. He was repeatedly elected to fill public positions, in the legislature and the like, and always acquitted himself with credit. In all good works he took his full share, and proved himself a liberal and public spirited citizen.

Remembering how much he was indebted for his own instruction to the English department in the Academy, he undoubtedly saw its discontinuance with regret. He therefore determined to devote a generous sum to its restoration. The trustees accepted his gift upon the conditions that he annexed to it, and the English course is now permanently reinstated in the school.

Mr. Odlin died the twenty-fourth of April. 1879, at the age of seventy-four.

HENRY WINKLEY is a son of William Winkley, of Barrington, where he was born in 1806 ; and lived upon his father's farm until he was twenty-one years of age. He then went to Boston "to seek his fortune," and obtained employment there from a dealer in crockery and china ware. He was afterwards engaged in the same business in New York, and finally in Philadelphia, where he became the chief of a large wholesale and importing house. About thirty years ago he retired from business, having been highly successful in the accumulation of property. Since then he has continued to make Philadelphia his residence, but has travelled extensively, in this country and in Europe. Within the few past years, he has distributed large sums of money among institutions of learning in New England.

The temptation to devote an extended chapter to the Alumni, is only controlled by the want of sufficient space. They number above five thousand, and represent nearly every State and Territory of the Union, besides a fair proportion of foreign countries. It would be an interesting task to enumerate those among them who have attained prominence in some of the various departments of human effort. The list would assuredly be a long one, and would include many men of national repute,—some whose fame has spread wherever civilization extends.

The Academy includes among her earlier sons, especially,

an extraordinary group of eminent men. That Webster and
Cass, Everett and Dix, Palfrey and Sparks and Bancroft
should have appeared at a single school in the space of fifteen years, is indeed wonderful. And yet, proud as Exeter
must be of these great names upon her roll, their greatness
cannot of course be attributed exclusively, or, indeed, in
any very great degree, to the effect of her training. No
doubt they profited much by the lessons of her able and
interested instructors and mentors, and found the rugged
pathway to learning made pleasanter, through the halls of
Exeter, and smoother to their feet. But men of their excep-
tional powers would have achieved eminence with any training—perhaps with no training.

A school is fairly to be judged by its fruits ; not by a few
isolated cases, but by what it has done for the great body
of those whom it has assumed to discipline and instruct.
The average scholarship of its pupils, their command of
their powers, their habits of application, their love for learning, their ambition to excel, their manly attributes, courtesy,
kindness, truthfulness and honor, are all elements to be
weighed in assigning to the school which nurtured them its
true place in the scale of merit. The judicious friends of
Phillips Exeter Academy, while making no claims of its
superiority over other admirable and better endowed schools,
are content to submit its pretensions to this test. And they
believe that the examination papers and merit rolls of our
colleges, and the records of our professional seminaries, as
well as a survey of those employments in the field of active
life in which thorough early training most tells, will show
that the men who have undergone Exeter drill, and formed
themselves by Exeter traditions, have taken places second
to those of the graduates of no other American school.

VI.

The Recreations.

It has been remarked that Exeter exhibits fewer class societies and other associations for diversion, than most other schools of equal magnitude. There is perhaps some truth in the statement; but it is not to be inferred from this circumstance that the students do not enjoy an abundance of recreations. Although the impress of work is visible everywhere, yet amusements receive, and have always received, their full share of attention from the school.

One of the earliest recreations of the students of which any record remains, was derived from the voluntary performance of military exercises. This began shortly before the close of the last century, and as Lewis Cass, then in the Academy, was prominent in the movement, it is not unlikely that he was one of the authors of it. This is rendered more probable by the fact that his father was at that time an officer on active duty in the army, and by the aptitude for the martial profession which the son subsequently evinced.

The first definite information that we have of a military organization in the school, is on the occasion of the obsequies of President Washington, in 1799. The land was filled with mourning, and every city and town and hamlet paid honor to his memory. The Legislature of New Hampshire was in session in Exeter, when the intelligence of his death was received. Resolutions of warm admiration for the virtue and patriotism of the deceased, and of profound sorrow for the country's bereavement, were adopted by both Houses, and it was voted that the Executive and the Legislature should jointly give their attendance at the religious exercises to be performed in the town, on the occasion.

Accordingly at the appointed hour, the Governor, attended by the Council, together with the Senate and House of Representatives, marched in solemn procession to the church, where appropriate religious services were held. The procession was preceded by "a military escort formed of the students of Phillips Exeter Academy, in uniform, with proper badges of mourning." Lewis Cass was the commander of the corps. And in acknowledgement of the service, the Legislature caused to be printed one hundred copies of Washington's Farewell Address, and of the record of their own action on this occasion, and ordered that a copy of the same should be given to each of the students of the Academy. A few copies of the publication,—a duodecimo of thirty-six pages,—are still extant.

The students' military corps, took to itself, perhaps from this occasion, the name of "the Washington Whites." The uniform adopted by its members consisted of a frock and pantaloons, doubtless of some white material, with a corresponding cockade and plume. The officers wore each an epaulet, the captain on the right shoulder, the subalterns on the left. The company usually numbered forty or fifty privates; the officers were a captain, three lieutenants, an ensign, four sergeants and a clerk. They ordinarily paraded in public three or four times in each year, and performed escort duty for the Trustees at their annual meetings. They appeared several years on the Fourth of July, when that anniversary was publicly observed in the town; and twice turned out to escort Gov. Gilman, and once to escort Gov. Smith, into town, on their return from "election."

The corps embraced, in the course of its existence, a goodly number of lads who grew in after life to be men of note. Three of these, at least, are still living; viz. George Kent,

Alpheus S. Packard and George Bancroft. Besides these, the
roster of the company bore the not unknown names of Nathaniel A. Haven, Jr., George Washington Storer, William
Plumer, Jr., James H. Duncan, Edward Everett, Charles
Folsom, William Willis, John S. Sleeper, John G. Palfrey,
William B. O. and Oliver W. B. Peabody, Richard Hildreth,
Jonathan P. Cushing and Gideon L. Soule.   President
Cushing was a captain, and Principal Soule a lieutenant;
and the latter used to describe with enthusiasm the excellent
drill and the soldierly appearance of the company, in its
palmy days.

The military ardor, which was probably kept alive by the
war of 1812, gradually declined after that was over, and by
the year 1818 had reached so low an ebb, that the organization of the Washington Whites was abandoned. And though
attempts were repeatedly made, in later years, to resuscitate
the company, they were attended with no lasting success.
When the Southern Rebellion broke out upon the country in
1861, the great body of the students, in common with the
youth of the entire North, formed themselves into drill-clubs,
and practiced the rudiments of the military art. Of course
the major part of them were too young to enter into actual
service, but a considerable number, who were of proper age,
marched from the school to join the Union army. They
were escorted, with every mark of honor, by their fellow
students, to the train which was to bear them to the field,
and departed amid the cheers and God-speeds of their companions.

A chapter of deep interest might be written upon Phillips
Exeter Academy in the war. Her gallant sons performed
their full share of patriotic service on every battle field;
many of them sealed their devotion to the cause of their
country with their life blood; and not a few attained high
command, and wrote their names by deeds of daring, and
by martial achievements, on the enduring pages of history.

With the dissolution of the military company in 1818, a

new subject arose, to turn the students' ideas into a more pacific channel. Under the encouragement of Professor Hildreth, the Golden Branch Society was instituted; and lads once ambitious only to excel in the exercises of the soldier, now panted to be admitted, with the chosen few, to the arcana of the new mystic fraternity.

The design of the society was the very commendable one of associating together the more diligent and aspiring of the students, for social and intellectual improvement. Its plan contemplated the election of new members by the society, from each successive class, in a certain ratio. For more than fifteen years the society went on, recruiting its numbers in this way, without difficulty. But as the election to membership came to be regarded as a desirable distinction, it is not strange, that, honestly as the power may have been exercised, jealousy and dissatisfaction sometimes manifested themselves among those who were left out. No overt demonstration of these feelings was made, however, until the year 1837. That was about the time when the anti-masonic excitement pervaded the community, and rendered wise men foolish, on the subject of secret associations; so that even the harmless Phi Beta Kappa society of our colleges was compelled in deference to the popular clamor, to surrender the dread secret hidden under its cabalistic initials.

This jealousy of secret societies manifested itself in the Academy by an organized opposition to the Golden Branch. A number of the students, some of them above the average standing, declared hostilities against the society, taking exception not only to its secrecy, but also to its arrogant pretentions in styling itself the *Golden* Branch, as if to imply that the remaining branches of the Academy were of inferior metal. They also complained of the arbitrary manner of choosing its members, and of their lack of courtesy to the other students.

Another society was formed by the malcontents, based, no doubt, on more liberal principles, and avowedly set up in opposition to the Golden Branch. The officers of the new society published in a pamphlet an address to the members of the old one, which being considered disrespectful in its tone to the authorities of the Academy, the offenders were removed from the school. A part of their number made such acknowledgements that they were allowed to return ; the others went their way. A reorganization of the Golden Branch was one of the results of the affair; and since that time it has maintained no such secrecy as to offend the most scrupulous.

The Golden Branch still flourishes, and occupies a room in the main Academy building. It holds its regular weekly meetings for literary exercises, and possesses a library of considerable size and value. It is not, however, the only society of its class in the Academy. Within a few years the G. L. Soule Literary Society has been established, and is in successful operation. A room in the Academy is assigned to this Society, also, where its meetings are held, and its library, now of respectable dimensions, is deposited.

In the earlier days of the Academy, games of marbles were much in vogue. The larger boys were then not above carrying their pockets full of the common yellow clay pellets which were the stakes of the game, with a few choice white, or striped "alleys," to be used as projectiles. It was not considered *infra dig.*, for even a senior to "knuckle down" to a game on the earthen sidewalk, and the cry of "no fudgings" was enough to restrain the most lawless from violating the rules of the ring. But marbles seem to be numbered with the things that were ; it is many years since they disappeared from the Academy.

Football and hand-ball have kept their place among the sports of the students from the very first; though the rules of play with them, have been much changed of late years. Half a century ago football was the simplest of games, and every boy in the school who was capable of running, could, and often did, take part in it. Some, of course, by natural

powers and by practice, acquired a great superiority over the
rest, but no student was so awkward or so unskilful that he
was debarred from playing.

The games of bat-and-ball in former years were various,
but the most popular were "four old cat" and base ball. The
latter alone survives to this day, and in a very changed condition. In these games, as in football, no special expert-
ness was then requisite to enable one to join. A very large
proportion of the students participated in the sport ; and the
old residents will readily recall·with what regularity Fast day
used to be devoted to the base ball of the period.

But those games have greatly changed their character in
latter days. The process of evolution has transformed the
simple into the complex, the easy into the difficult, the
healthful recreation into a *tour de force*. No more are these
amusements open to the whole school ; they are now practically confined to a small number of picked and. trained
athletes. It is not an edifying spectacle to a man of old-
fashioned prejudices, to see half a score of muscular young
fellows, in fantastic costumes, having all the play (if such
tough work can be called by that name) to themselves, while
a hundred or two of their school fellows sit around the campus, during a whole afternoon, with no other occupation than
to gaze at them. If the purpose of school games is, as it
has generally been thought to be, to furnish amusement combined with healthful exercise, it certainly seems that those
should be preferred, which do "the greatest good to the
greatest number." And it is a satisfaction to see that a
reaction has apparently begun in the school, and that
games are now introduced, in which every boy, without special training, can join, and have his share of fun, and of action
as well.

The English public school game of "hare and hounds"
has been occasionally attempted at Exeter, but not with
entirely satisfactory results. Neither the climate nor the
face of the country is so well adapted for it here, as in Eng-

land. Moreover the violent exercise of running, over considerable distances, has never been practiced in this country to any great extent.

Boating has become a rather popular amusement for a number of years past. The "salt river" affords an opportunity for excellent practice. A boat club is maintained in the Academy, crews are carefully selected, and coached after the approved method. Their boats are the work of the best builders, and it is an inspiring sight to watch the crews pulling, with their measured stroke, up and down the channel. Boating, however, as it is at present conducted, though it furnishes excellent exercise, is too expensive an amusement to be generally indulged in.

The bicycle, too, is a rather costly machine, and its use is therefore somewhat limited. This is not to be regretted, for though as a means of locomotion it is rapid, and enables one to take an airing with facility, yet as a method of obtaining bodily exercise it is very defective. The lower limbs, no doubt, have enough of it, but the constrained position of the upper part of the body cannot but be injurious. No one desires to become round shouldered or flat chested, even if he is satisfied with the abnormal muscular development of a kangaroo.

Exeter has never been disgraced by the practice of "hazing." In former times, there were certain ordeals which new comers were obliged to undergo, but they were only rough, never brutal. Two of them are alluded to by the venerable Col. George Kent, in his versified account of the sports of Exeter, three-fourths of a century ago.* One of these was "shinning up" a bare post in the Academy; and though this would have been only a pastime to those light active boys, who seem to climb as naturally as squirrels, yet it must have been a serious trial to some of the clumsy ones.

"Scrubbing" was the other ordeal. When the first snow of the winter came, every new boy had to be washed in it,

*Appendix K.

If he was a wise urchin he submitted to the operation kindly, and escaped with a comparatively gentle handling. But if he resisted, so much the worse for him. A dozen strong arms held him fast, while his face was diligently scrubbed with the newly fallen flakes (not unmixed with sand or gravel) until the unfortunate wight, with tingling cuticle, and eyes full of tears, was fain to beg for mercy.

Winter was the season of many amusements. Skating on the river, and coasting, especially when the snow was covered with a crust that would bear the weight of a boy and sled, were favorite pastimes. Snowballing, in former times, was not confined to the occasions when a fresh downfall or a thaw rendered the snow temptingly plastic, but was a business that lasted the season through. Forts of solid frostwork used to be erected, which were the objects of attack and defence, in a very creditable imitation of genuine warfare.

There is a tradition of one snow fort in particular, built not very long after the termination of the last war with Great Britain, which was of unprecedented strength and magnitude. On its lofty battlements a sentinel student kept watch and ward by night and by day, lest the hostile town boys should capture it by a sudden onslaught. A bell crowned its summit, to sound an alarm to the garrison, should danger threaten. Every student felt in honor bound to do his duty manfully as a defender of this citadel of his order. A store of ammunition was provided in the form of snow balls, soaked in water and frozen to ice, so that when impelled by stalwart arms, they were little less to be dreaded than veritable bullets.

Perhaps this eternal vigilance and these bellicose preparations impressed the town boys with a wholesome dread of assaulting a work as apparently impregnable, in which they were likely to get more bruises than glory ; on that subject tradition is silent. But the fort if it were ever captured, was not demolished. Through the long winter it stood in mim-

paired solidity ; the gentler breath of spring failed to sap its
icy foundations ; and even summer, with its sunshine and
tropical showers, seemed for a while powerless to cope with
this frosted monument of stern winter's reign ; so that it was
not till the sultry heats of July, that its last vestiges disappeared.

And then it was found that from the spot where those too
solid walls had stood, every trace of vegetation had van-
ished. All that remained to tell where the great snow fort
had been reared, was a wide circular tract of dead sand, in
the midst of the beautiful greenery of the Academy yard.
Nor did the memory of the icy fortress perish in a single
year. Springs came and summers went, and still no blade
of grass enlivened the dull gray of that charmed circle where
once stood the memorable structure. Every new boy, as he
wonderingly inquired the cause of this strange phenomenon,
listened *arrectis auribus*, to the strange explanation furnished by his more sophisticated companions, and gazed
upon this indisputable evidence of departed glories, with the
interest and with the faith, of a juvenile Schliemann.

This chapter might be indefinitely prolonged. The rec-
ollections of the "old boys" would afford the materials
for a volume, upon the pastimes of former generations of
pupils ; and an abstract of the contents of "the Pean,"
would disclosed the number of secret societies known by
Greek initials, of associations for religious, political, literary,
musical and various other purposes of amusement and improvement, which the students at this time maintain ; among
which, and worthy of special mention, is the list of editors
of "the Exonian," a newspaper for several years past issued
weekly during term time, devoted to college and academy
news, and conducted with marked ability, taste and judgment.

But these things would swell this sketch far beyond its
allotted size ; and an allusion to one pleasant custom of the
Academy, now for many years fallen into desuetude, must
bring it to a close.

The annual exhibitions of the Academy were formerly occasions of great interest to the school and to the town and vicinity. For them elaborate preparations were made; and the number of delighted spectators was limited only by the capacity of the Academy hall. Ushers, of resolution, and of muscle, too, were indispensable to repress the eagerness of outsiders to rush in before the dignitaries had been decorously placed in the seats of honor assigned to them, as well as to preserve order during the performance of the exercises. Every youth who was honored with a part, entertained a full sense of his importance; and the audience regarded "the Doctor," at whose nod the exercises proceeded, as if he were, as indeed in a sense he was, the monarch of all he surveyed.

It is interesting to scan the old "orders of exercises," at those exhibitions. The very earliest ones, in which might probably be found the names of some of those whose subsequent career reflected most luster upon the Academy, are not now to be found. In that of seventy-six years ago, the "Salutatory Oration in Latin" was assigned to Edward Everett, and a part also to Nathaniel H. Carter, whose premature death precluded the complete fulfilment of his early promise. In the exhibition of 1814, Jonathan P. Cushing and Gideon L. Soule took part; and in 1818 "a Poem" was recited by Thomas W. Dorr, afterwards noted for his connection with the popular movement in Rhode Island which in 1842 was termed rebellion, but would probably be thought deserving of a milder designation, at present. In 1822 appeared Richard Hildreth, of literary and historic fame; in 1823 Alpheus Crosby the learned professor, John P. Hale the eminent advocate and Senator, and John H. Warland the poet editor, whose abilities have scarcely received due recognition.

In the later orders of exercises a greater number of names are met with, which happily are not yet "starred." And in 1825 and 1826 are found those of Charles W. Woodman, Luther D. Sawyer and Hamilton E. Perkins, who, notwithstanding considerably more than half a century has passed over their whitening heads since they performed upon the stage of Exeter, are confidently expected to unite, with their seniors as well as their juniors, in celebrating, with all their youthful enthusiasm. the centennial birthday of Phillips Exeter Academy.

Appendix.

A, page 6.

LETTER FROM JOHN PHILLIPS TO MRS. JOSIAH GILMAN.

Andover, December 17, 1765.

My Dear Mrs. Gilman: I am almost charmed with the beautiful and animated lines with which you have favored me. I have been ardently wishing for your dear grandmother's picture, and you make me happy in presenting me therewith. Methinks the lovely person lives in you, and that the old mansion house is once more enlivened and ornamented with the living image of its late inhabitant. Your fondness for my return minds me of her anxiety for me when absent, and the sweet welcome which her faithful heart discovered in her countenance, as well as with her lips, when she received me. Her tender concern, quick sensibility and just resentment upon the appearance of anything injurious to my person or character, your feeling heart has dictated, and your ready pen described in the most lively manner.

But I forbear; I consider you are yet living, and may you live long to make my friend happy in your copying after an example which it is your laudable ambition to imitate.

I take this opportunity to express my thankfulness for the favor I obtained of the Lord when the wife of my youth gave her hand with her heart to so unworthy a person, who appears to himself to have been but as a foil to make her excellence more resplendent. He who kindly gave, hath taken. I bless his name—but my breast heaves—my heart still bleeds; the image is too deeply impressed to be effaced. Is she dead? Oh, she yet speaks; her works speak for her; her Sarah rises up and calls her blessed. Her husband, also, (whilst he laments his own grievous failings) praiseth her and praiseth God for his undeserved goodness in blessing him with such a consort—a consort so amiable, cheerful, fru-

gal, wise, prudent, peaceable. meek, modest, neat. diligent.
careful, contented, of such steady conduct, strict virtue and
exemplary piety, so apparent in the constant discharge of the
various duties of the Christian life—and in the prospect of
death how remarkable serene and submissive to the will of her
Father which is now done. And what remains but that we
also be subject to his will, and have our conversation where
we doubt not she is, and endeavor to become followers
of Christ as she was, and followers of her and all those
who, through faith and patience. are gone to inherit the
promise. May her offspring be the blessed of the Lord. and
her and my dear namesakes find their names written in the
Lamb's book of life.

Which is the prayer of

Your ever loving.

J. P.

B, page 11.

LETTERS OF JOHN PHILLIPS TO HIS BROTHERS.

To Samuel Phillips.

Exeter, May 24, 1762.

Dear Brother : As I hear you are relieved from a part of
public business, which necessarily engrossed much of your
time and attention, you have now more leisure to employ
your thoughts and cares upon the very important proposal
you made, of a united effort in our family, for doing some
special service for God. Pray let me know Father's and
Brother's thoughts thereon, and what your present appre-
hension is.

It appears by a public advertisement there is a new Society incorporated at Boston for the purpose which, you remem-
ber I told you, laid most upon my mind. Pray write me
what to you has an encouraging or discouraging aspect upon
that scheme. Our parents designed and educated us to serve
Christ personally in the work of the ministry ; our time has
been otherwise employed ; our other labors by his blessing
succeeded. May our God have the fruits of them for the
carrying to an end the same blessed work by such whom he
shall please to send.

(Extract) To William Phillips.

Exeter, June 2, 1762.

I would gladly know who was chose President and who are

the principal members of a Society lately incorporated in Boston for sending the gospel among the heathen, (as I suppose, having only seen an advertisement in the Boston paper,) whether the gentlemen who are at the expense of this service belong to this country or Great Britain ; to what nations or tribes are the missions, and who the missionaries. I am the more inquisitive as I apprehend a service of this nature is of the utmost importance, and, if under due regulations, ought to be greatly encouraged, not only by particular persons, but by the several governments, since Heaven has granted us such marvellous successes.

Has Christ subdued our enemies around us, and shall we not unite our endeavors to bring them under his yoke? Gratitude, my Brother, gratitude to our beneficent Lord requires it ; compassion for the souls of our fellow-creatures calls for it. Was there ever a more open door, or a people less excusable if so great a work (heretofore too much neglected) should not now be generally promoted, with cheerfulness and zeal?

C, page 14.

EPITAPH ON THE FOUNDER.

JOHN PHILLIPS, LL. D.

Founder of the Phillips Exeter Academy.
An Associate Founder of the Phillips Academy in Andover,
And a liberal benefactor of Dartmouth College,
Died
April 21, 1795
aged 75 years.
Actuated by his ardent attachment to the cause of Christianity
He devoted his wealth to the advancement of
Letters and Religion.
His appropriate monument are
The institutions which bear his name.

D, page 22.

While preparing these sheets for the press the writer was favored by the Hon. Mellen Chamberlain, of Boston, with a bundle of old bills incurred by the three sons of Mr. Moses Grant, while attending the Academy in the years 1798 and 1799. They boarded in the family of Deacon Samuel Brooks, a highly respectable citizen of the town, at the cost of $2 per week, which apparently included lodging and washing also They were under the charge of Mr. Peter Thacher, Jr., who is presumed to have been the same person whose name now appears in the catalogue as an instructor in 1796 with the middle initial of "O," and was afterwards the Judge of the Municipal Court of Boston.

Next to the board bill, the largest item is for dancing lessons given by M. Renard, being $35 for a year's instruction. It appears, therefore, that in those early days of the Academy, dancing was not considered incompatible with study. The only books mentioned as purchased in Exeter, are Latin Grammars, Æsop's Fables, Morse's Geography, Young's and Entick's Dictionaries, and the Village Harmony. "Bunches of quills," and "papers of ink powder" among the items, remind us of the difficulties under which our grandfathers had to labor in order to obtain the materials for writing their beautiful and elaborate letters. A charge for "tackling the skates" shows that the students of that day practiced the exhilerating exercise of skating on the river; while "cash to Mrs. Taylor for making a uniform" carries us back to the primitive age,—long since outgrown,—when youngsters did not disdain to allow their garments to be fashioned by women.

E, page 26.

There is preserved among the papers of the Academy a list of the students who were awarded prizes, during the eight years that this vote of the Trustees continued in force. The number varied in different years, from eight in 1809 to two in 1813. Two of the recipients, at least, are still living; George Kent, who in 1809 was adjudged entitled to three dollars for the highest improvement, made among the members of certain specified classes, in Latin and Greek, "particular regard being had to accuracy and correctness;" and George Bancroft who in 1812 carried off the prize of four dollars, as "the scholar who most distinguished himself in construing and parsing the Greek and Latin languages." His reward appears to have been given him in the form of a book, "Elements of Criticism;" and it may be inferred from his subsequent career that he made a good use of it.

A few of the written exercises prepared for competition have been preserved, evidently on account of the beauty of their execution. They are specimens of Latin composition; and while we may fairly hope that the students of our own time can boast an equal proficiency in the language, yet we despair of ever again seeing in the Academy such perfect calligraphy. Three of the pieces are the work of lads who carried the same habits of carefulness and finish, if not the same beautiful penmanship, into the work of their later years. by which their names have been rendered famous, viz: Charles Folsom, John G. Palfrey and Jared Sparks.

F, page 29.

LIST OF STUDIES, ADOPTED IN 1818, IN THE ACADEMY.

CLASSICAL DEPARTMENT.

For the First Year:

Adam's Latin Grammar; Liber Primus, or a similar work; Viri Romani, or Cæsar's Commentaries; Latin Prosody; Exercises in Reading and making Latin; Ancient and Modern Geography; Virgil and Arithmetic.

For the Second Year:

Virgil; Arithmetic and Exercises in Reading and making Latin, continued; Valpey's Greek Grammar; Roman History; Cicero's Select Orations; Delectus; Dalzel's Collectanea Græca Minora; Greek Testament; English Grammar and Declamation.

For the Third Year:

The same Latin and Greek authors in revision; English Grammar and Declamation continued; Sallust; Algebra; Exercises in Latin and English translations, and Composition.

For the Advanced Class:

Collectanea Græca Majora; Q. Horatius Flaccus; Titus Livius; Parts of Terence's Comedies; Excerpta Latina, or such Latin and Greek authors as may best comport with the student's future destination; Algebra; Geometry; Elements of Ancient History; Adam's Roman Antiquities, etc.

ENGLISH DEPARTMENT.

For admission into this department the candidate must be at least twelve years of age, and must have been well instructed in Reading and Spelling; familiarly acquainted with Arithmetic, through Simple Proportion with the exception of Fractions, with Murray's English Grammar through Syntax, and must be able to parse simple English sentences.

The following is the course of instruction and study in the English Department, which with special exceptions, will comprise three years.

For the First Year:

English Grammar including exercises in Reading, in Parsing and Analyzing, in the correction of bad English; Punctuation and Prosody; Arithmetic; Geography, and Algebra through Simple Equations.

For the Second Year:

English Grammar continued; Geometry; Plane Trigonometry and its application to heights and distances; mensuration of Sup. and Sol.; Elements of Ancient History; Logic; Rhetoric; English Composition; Declamation and exercises of the Forensic kind.

For the Third Year:

Surveying; Navigation; Elements of Chemistry and Natural Philosophy, with experiments; Elements of Modern History, particularly of the United States; Moral and Political Philosophy, with English Composition, Forensics and Declamation continued.

G, page 30.

DR. ABBOTS' LETTER OF RESIGNATION.

To the honorable Board of Trustees of Phillips Exeter Academy:

Gentlemen:—It is now fifty years since under your direction I commenced the government and instruction of Phillips Exeter Academy. Age and infirmity admonish me that it is time to retire from a scene of labor and responsibility which is better suited to an earlier period of life, and may be more successfully sustained by younger men. At the close of this long period of active service it is a satisfaction to me that I leave the institution where my strongest sympathies and uninterrupted labors have been employed, in a comparatively prosperous condition.

If in any measure the objects of the pious Founder have been attained, and the reasonable expectations of the public satisfied, much is to be attributed to union in counsel and the constant aid and support of the Trustees,—and I cannot on this occasion omit to express my grateful obligation to the Board whose uniform kindness and courtesy I have ever experienced, and which have greatly contributed to alleviate the toils and anxieties of a long life.

I have now, gentlemen, to repeat the desire that my connexion with the institution as Principal may terminate at the end of the present term, and that a successor be appointed to supply the place. And at the close of my labors permit me to express my best wishes for your personal happiness, and to assure you of the continuance of my fervent prayers for the future prosperity of the institution.

> With great respect and affection,
>
> I am your obedient servant,
>
> BENJAMIN ABBOT.

RESOLUTION OF THE TRUSTEES.

Voted, unanimously, that the Trustees cannot accept the resignation, as they now do, of a long tried officer without expressing their deep regret at the dissolution of the connection which has so long and so happily subsisted between them. It is now fifty years since Dr. Abbot was placed, in the lifetime of the Founder, at the head of the instruction of this Academy. It is personally known to some of the present members of the Board that the Founder, during the remaining seven years of his life, entirely approved the conduct of the Principal, as did also those who have successively exercised the office of governors and visitors of this Academy.

The endowment of this charity is believed to be among the most ample and liberal of its class in the United States, and for that reason talents and qualifications rarely found united in one man were required in the person charged with the instruction and government. A clear and sound understanding,—talents beyond the ordinary rate for acquiring, and aptness in communicating instruction,—an enlarged knowledge of human nature,—sagacity to discern the characters, capacities and dispositions of youth, accompanied by a mild and equable temper and disposition of mind,—suavity of manners and above all a kind and affectionate heart,—ready at all times to put on the parent,—regarding his pupils as children entrusted by Providence to his care,—all these qualities and many others adapted to his situation, experience has shown were happily blended in the man of their choice. The present Trustees and many of their predecessors can claim no merit in the appointment (that merit is chiefly to be ascribed to the Founder) but only in a disposition duly to appreciate the merits and conduct of their Principal, and steadily to support his authority,—to adopt such plans and measures for instruction and government as experience should have suggested to him as necessary and useful,—and the uniform disposition to make his situation as easy and comfortable to him on the means placed at their disposal would allow. The records of the Academy abundantly show that the most cordial and affectionate confidence has ever subsisted between the governors and visitors of the charity and the important officer charged with its internal direction and management.

It gives the Trustees unfeigned pleasure to believe that this school has proved, and has been ever so regarded, as one of the best in our country, and for the whole period of Dr. Abbot's superintendence, assisted as he has generally been by young men of superior talents and liberal minds, has sent forth scholars and gentlemen distinguished for their classical knowledge and scientific attainments, some of whom have completed their studies here. This furnishes the best evidence of the usefulness of the institution and of the merits of its instructors.

The Trustees cannot but ascribe much of the excellence of this school, and its present well digested and matured rules and usages, to the prudence and caution of its Principal,— avoiding on the one hand all rash and hasty experiments in the delicate business of education, and on the other, evincing a constant readiness to avail himself of the new lights shed upon this branch of knowledge at home and abroad. It has been attempted here to lay the foundations deep and broad, and to dispense none but correct and accurate instruction in all the branches taught, and as far as our sphere extends, to make solid rather than shining scholars.

The Trustees have thus thought it to be a duty they owed their late Principal to advert in brief terms to the course of education pursued in this Academy for the last twenty-five years, and to express their full and entire approbation, and also their determination to continue it. They flatter themselves that the intentions and hopes of the benevolent Founder have been thus far, and will continue to be, realized.

The Trustees in taking leave of their Principal, earnestly pray that the decline of his now advanced years may be as serene and happy as his long and faithful services have been productive of the happiness and improvement of others. His retrospection cannot fail to afford him the truest felicity. They hope he will long live to see and enjoy the good fruits of his laborious and well spent life.

II, page 31.

SONG, FOR THE ABBOT JUBILEE.
Tune, "Auld Lang Syne."

When after toil and wanderings long
  In many a distant land,
Around a father's hearth is met
  Once more the household band,
How gratefully ascend the notes
  Of mingled joy and praise;
While, sadly sweet, the thought returns
  Of happy early days.

And here, a band of grateful sons,
  We, too, to-day have met,
To bless the kind, paternal care
  We never can forget;—
To bless the hand that guided us
  In Learning's pleasant ways,
And led us to the springs of Truth,
  In those, our early days.

How fresh to-day come back the light
  And air of those bright years
When life and hope were young, and yet
  Undimmed by cares or fears.
Then, with united hearts and voice,
  Together let us raise
One song of joy, to celebrate
  Our happy, early days.

Each voice be raised, each eye, to bless
  Our Guide, Instructor, Friend;
May Heaven's best gifts still wait upon
  His life, till life shall end.
And may the tribute that we bring
  Of filial love and praise
Bind, with a crown of light, his brow,
  Who blessed our early days.

SONG, WRITTEN FOR THE FESTIVAL AT EXETER,
AUGUST 23, 1838.

O'er the blue depths of ocean the mariner's sail
Like the wing of the sea bird, is bent to the gale,
And the sunbeam is glancing in light on the foam
As hurries the tempest-tossed wanderer home.
Away with each weary remembrance of pain,
As he crosses the dearly loved threshold again!
Some faces are absent, once radiant and fair,
But the welcome and smile of a Parent are there.

And well may our hearts with fond memories burn,
To the scenes of past joys as once more we return;
Kind voices are silent,—warm bosoms are chill,—
But the friend of our infancy welcomes us still!
The Friend, who once guided the steps of our youth

Along the bright pathway of learning and truth;
Cold, cold must those hearts be, those memories dim,
When they kindle no more with affection for him!

Too soon will this hour of enjoyment be gone;
Then, as the sad moment of parting steals on,
Let us breathe one kind wish for his welfare, before
We wander, perhaps to behold him no more.
Be the mild light of peace on his eventide shed,
And light fall the sorrows of age on his head!
May each blessing that friendship and gratitude cast
On the pathway of virtue, be his to the last!

I, page 43.

HON. GEORGE S. HALE'S POEM.

I.

The young Iulus, midst the Trojan fire,
With steps unequal, followed his great sire,
His wandering o'er, the patriotic boy
Helped to build up another, greater Troy.

II.

With steps unequal tho' we follow those
Whose wide spread fame each proud Alumnus knows,
Who made the glory of the days gone by,
And lived conspicuous in the Nation's eye.

III.

Perchance our second Troy shall bear our fame
To future ages with some greater name,
Our Hector by some Cæsar—be outdone,
And Webster's glory have some greater son.

IV.

Dear are the memories of the ancient shrine,
Who is not glad to say "And these were mine!"
The morning greetings in the noisy Hall—,
The jovial crowd that chased the flying ball.

V.

The rare events when boyish hands, set free,
Clapped for a bride or birth with eager glee—
The hour reluctant, given to the broom
When Smith Secundus swept the Latin room.

VI.

The happy wanderings when spring was new,
The happy holidays that swiftly flew,
The record which we longed, yet feared to see
That told our parents what their boys might be.

VII.

But hours there are that graver thoughts employ,

Signs of the man fast growing in the boy;
The hours of study and the thoughts of fame,
Stirred by the memories of some honored name.

VIII.

For some the counting of the scanty store,
The anxious question, where to look for more,
How best to share of others' weary toil
And constant struggle with the ungrateful soil.

IX.

Oh! may these walls, we dedicate anew,
Still to the memories of the Past be true;
May sons succeeding sires still hold
The lengthening chain that binds the young and old.

X.

Still learn the lessons that their fathers learned
Win brighter honors than their fathers earned,
And crown the latter house their fathers raise,
With glory greater than the former days.

J, page 62.

LIST OF OFFICERS AND INSTRUCTORS.

TRUSTEES.

1781	Hon. John Phillips, LL. D.,	1795
1781	Hon. Samuel Phillips, LL.D.,	1802
1781	Thomas Odiorne,	1794
1781	Hon. John Pickering, LL.D,	1802
1781	Rev. David McClure, D.D.,	1787
1781	Rev. Benjamin Thurston,	1801
1781	Daniel Tilton,	1783
1783	William Woodbridge, A.M., *ex officio*	1788
1787	Hon. Paine Wingate, A.M.,	1809
1791	Benjamin Abbot, LL.D., *ex officio*	1838
1794	Hon. Oliver Peabody, A.M.,	1828
1795	Hon. John Taylor Gilman, LL.D.,	1827
1801	Rev. Joseph Buckminster, D.D.,	1812
1802	Rev. Jesse Appleton, D.D.,	1803
1809	Hon. John Phillips, A.M.,	1820
1802	Rev. Daniel Dana, D.D.,	1843
1809	Hon. Nathaniel Appleton Haven, A.M.,	1830
1812	Rev. Jacob Abbot, A.M.,	1831
1821	Rev. Nathan Parker, D.D.,	1833
1828	Hon. Jeremiah Smith, LL.D.,	1842
1831	Samuel Hale, A. M.,	1869
1834	Hon. Samuel Dana Bell, LL.D.,	1838
1835	Hon. Daniel Webster, LL.D.,	1852
1835	Rev. Charles Burroughs, D.D.,	1867
1838	Benjamin Abbot, LL. D.,	1844
1838	Gideon Lane Soule, A.M., *ex officio*,	1873

1842	Hon. James Bell, A.B.,	1852
1843	Rev. Andrew Preston Peabody, D.D.,	
1844	David Wood Gorham, A.B., M.D.,	1873
1853	Hon. Amos Tuck, A.M.,	1879
1853	Francis Bowen, A.M.,	1875
1868	Hon. Jeremiah Smith, A.M.,	1874
1870	Hon. George Silsbee Hale, A.B.,	
1873	Albert Cornelius Perkins, Ph.D., *ex officio*,	
1874	William Henry Gorham, M.D.,	1879
1874	Joseph Burbeen Walker, A.M.,	
1875	Rev. Phillips Brooks, D.D.,	1880
1879	Nicholas Emery Soule, A.M., M.D.,	
1879	Hon. Charles Henry Bell, LL.D.,	
1881	John Charles Phillips, A.B.,	

TREASURERS.

1781	Thomas Odiorne,	1793
1793	Hon. John Taylor Gilman, LL.D.,	1806
1806	Hon. Oliver Peabody, A.M.,	1828
1828	Hon. Jeremiah Smith, LL.D.,	1842
1842	Hon. John Kelly, A.M.,	1855
1855	Joseph Taylor Gilman,	1862
1862	S. Clarke Buzell,	1880
1880	Charles Burley,	

PRINCIPAL INSTRUCTORS

1783	William Woodbridge, A.M., *Preceptor*,	1788
1788	Benjamin Abbot, LL.D., *Principal*,	1838
1838	Gideon Lane Soule, LL.D., "	1873
1873	Albert Cornelius Perkins, Ph.D., *Principal*,	

INSTRUCTORS.

The collegiate degrees of the Instructors and Assistant Instructors, are those which they had received at the time of their several appointments.

1808	Ebenezer Adams, A.M., *Prof. Math. and Nat. Phil.*,	1809
1811	Hosea Hildreth, A.M., *Prof. Math. and Nat. Phil.*,	1825
1817	Rev. Isaac Hurd, A.M., *Theological Instructor*,	1839
1822	Gideon Lane Soule, A.M., *Prof. Ant. Languages*,	1838
1825	John Parker Cleaveland, A.B., *Prof. Math. and Nat. Phil.*,	1826
1826	Charles C. P. Gale, A.B., *Prof. Math. and Nat. Phil.*	1827
1827	Joseph Hale Abbot, A.M., *Prof. Math. and Nat. Phil.*	1833
1833	Francis Bowen, A.B., *Prof. Math. and Nat. Phil.*,	1835
1835	William Henry Shackford, A.B., *Prof. Math. and Nat. Phil.*,	1842
1836	Henry French, A.B., *Instructor in Languages*,	1840
1840	Nehemiah Cleaveland, A.M., *Prof. Ant. Languages*,	1841
1841	Joseph Gibson Hoyt, A.M., *Prof. Mathematics*,	1859
1842	Richard Wenman Swan, A. B., *Prof. Ant. Languages*	1851
1851	Paul Ansel Chadbourne, A.M., *Prof. Ant. Languages*	1852
1852	Theodore Tibbets, A.B., *Prof. Ant. Languages*,	1853
1853	Henry Stedman Nourse, A.B., *Prof. Ant. Languages*	1855

1855	George Carleton Sawyer, A.B., *Prof. Ant. Languages*	1858
1858	George Albert Wentworth, A.B., *Prof. Mathematics.*	
1859	Bradbury Longfellow Cilley, A.B., *Prof. Ant. Languages*	
1875	Robert Franklin Pennell, A.B., *Prof. Latin*	1882

ASSISTANT INSTRUCTORS.

1781	Joseph Willard, A.B.,	1785
1785	Salmon Chase, A.B.,	1786
1789	Joseph Dana, A.B.,	1789
1789	Daniel Dana, A.B.,	1791
1791	John Phillips Ripley, A.B,	1791
1792	Rufus Anderson, A.B.,	1792
1792	Abiel Abbot, A.B.,	1793
1793	Charles Coffin, A.B.,	1794
1794	Joseph Perkins, A.B.,	1795
1795	Timothy Winn, A.B.,	1796
1796	Peter Oxenbridge Thacher, A.B.,	1797
1797	Nicholas Emery, A.B,	1797
1797	George Wingate, A.B ,	1797
1797	William Craig, A.B.,	1799
1799	Samuel Dunn Parker, A.B.,	1800
1799	Horatio Gates Burnap, A.B.,	1803
1801	Joseph Stevens Buckminster, A.B.,	1803
1803	Samuel Willard, A. B.,	1804
1804	John Stickney, A. B.,	1805
1804	Ashur Ware, A. B.,	1805
1805	Martin Luther Hurlbut., A. B.,	1805
1805	Nathan Hale, A.B.,	1807
1806	Jaazaniah Crosby, A.B.,	1807
1806	Alexander Hill Everett, A. B.,	1807
1807	Nathaniel Appleton Haven, Jr. A.B.,	1808
1808	Reuben Washburn, A.B.,	1809
1809	Nathaniel Whitman A.B.,	1810
1810	Nathan Lord, A.B.,	1811
1810	Jonas Wheeler, A.B.,	1811
1811	Henry Holton Fuller, A.B.,	1812
1812	Henry Ware, A.B.,	1814
1814	James Walker, A.B.,	1815
1815	George Goldthwaite Ingersoll, A.B.,	1816
1816	William Bourne Oliver Peabody, A.B.,	1817
1817	Oliver William Bourne Peabody, A.B ,	1818
1818	Gideon Lane Soule, A.B.,	1819
1819	Samuel Taylor Gilman, A.B.,	1820
1820	Charles Lane Folsom, A B.,	1822
1856	Jacob Abbot Cram,	1857
1857	William Francis Bennett Jackson,	1857
1860	Orlando Marcellus Fernald,	1861
1861	Payson Merrill,	1862
1870	William Harrington Putnam, A. M.	1871
1871	Robert Franklin Pennell, A. B.,	1875
1874	Oscar Faulhaber, Ph. D.	

K. page

Poetical response, by Col. George Kent, to an inquiry respecting the games in use by the students, in 1807, when he was a member of the Academy.

I'm asked to say something of games and of sports,
That enjoyed the attention of youth of all sorts,
From the boy of thirteen to the man of two score
As wise at that age, in his own view, as more.
From Hawkes, Briggs and Sparks and from Piper and Capron,
Down to us hardly fresh from our infantile apron,
There were customs initial not much to our boast,
Such as forcing new comers to climb a bare post,
"Shin up" without aid until reaching the top
Of a pillar constructed the ceiling to prop,
Of the big room in old Academical Hall,
Whose desks and walls answered to many a scrawl.
A "washing" and scrubbing the face of new comer
Was also in vogue at the end of each summer,
Prostrating the form in the first sheet of snow
That might give, of the winter, the veriest show,
Through dint of the scrubbing unless by rare grace,
Leaving scarce to recumbent his primitive face.

But pastimes and games of a much better sort
Lent aid to our out door and innocent sport,
Such as marbles and foot ball, cat, cricket and base,
With occasional variance by a foot race.
In manner old-fashioned, and not through change fickle,
Knowing naught of rotation of modern bicycle.
And no flying of kites, such as stock markets show,
Where the process is often "a word and a blow,"—
A blow-up that ends in a sky-high disaster,
"Bulls" or "bears" left the victors, as each may be master.

But why of these matters presume thus to tell,
When all is already "as clear as a Bell,"
To my honored friend living just by the same spot,
Where early in life my crude views I thus got!
To some great extent games obey the same rules,
As, in spring, the same alewives seem gathered in schools
Many games that at present in vogue may be found,
Have been by long practice "run into the ground."
In naught I can say could I further enlighten
Or by *old* reminiscences, *new* intellects brighten;
So with *this* rambling scribble, you will please be content
And this tribute accept from your true friend
                              GEORGE KENT.

Washington, D. C., May, 1883.

Contents.